A Voice in the Wilderness
Volume 11

A Final Call

Dalen Garris

This is a work of history. Historical individuals and places and events are mentioned.

Copyright © 2022 by Dalen Garris

Published by Revivalfire Ministries

Cover design by Renee Garris

ISBN 13: 978-1-7377944-6-2

All rights reserved.
No part of this book may be used or reproduced in any manner whatsoever, without written permission, except in the case of brief quotations embodied in critical articles and reviews, as provided by U.S. Copyright Law.

For information, address
dale@revivalfire.org

First paperback printing January 2022

Printed in the United States of America

"Blow ye the trumpet in Zion, and sound an alarm in my holy mountain:
Let all the inhabitants of the land tremble: for the day of the LORD cometh, for it is nigh at hand"

Joel 2:1

Contents

Introduction	1
Elijah's Walk in the Desert	3
Two Paths Diverged in a Yellow Wood	9
African Prayer Meetings	13
The Great Danger of Modern Christianity	17
Too Tough for Demas	23
Dissolving Hymenaeus	27
Evidence	31
Hope	35
Saving Nineveh	37
The Effectiveness of Charles Spurgeon	41
Battleground	45
The Theology of Prayer	49
Agonizomai	51
Releasing Praise	57
Trust in God	61
Touch Not My Anointed	65
Gratitude on the Beach	69

The Garments of Humility	73
Calvinism and the Issue of Blood	77
Blood, Fire, Fear, and Souls of Men	81
Sons of Sceva	89
What is the Fullness of Joy?	93
Daniel's Final Mission	97
Camper for Sale	103
"What, Me Worry?"	107
Cain and Abel	111
Gilbert Tennent by David Smithers	115
Where is the Wise?	119
Drench the Sacrifice	125
Under a Bushel	131
By the Brook Cherith	135

Introduction

This volume may very well be the last in this series. Just as the passage in Isaiah calls out for a voice in the wilderness, so have I also hoped to use these compilations of the articles as a voice to wake the Church out of a slumber that she has slowly drifted into over the past few generations. She doesn't see it in herself but rather rustles up her skirts in pride whenever it is pointed out to her. She sees herself as Esther but is more like the widow of Zarepath.

Revival is truly coming, but the path that leads to it will be hard. Along with the persecution we are told that we will face in these coming last days, there will have to be a time of deep, broken repentance before the Church is ready to receive the outpouring that is coming.

A Voice in the Wilderness is just that – a voice that is crying to make the paths straight again to prepare the way for the coming of this Great Endtime Revival, the greatest revival of all time, and for the advent of our long-awaited Savior.

We are quickly approaching what may be the Church's final call.

Elijah's Walk in the Desert

And the angel of the LORD came again the second time, and touched him, and said, Arise and eat; because the journey is too great for thee.
And he arose, and did eat and drink, and went in the strength of that meat forty days and forty nights unto Horeb the mount of God. (1 Kings 19:7,8)

Over two hundred miles, maybe more, depending on where Mt. Horeb was and how circuitous a route he took. Forty days walking. That's a long, lonely walk.

Although prophets of God do not lead normal lives like most people, there can be glimpses of our own walks with God in them. You may not have called fire down from Heaven, but you do the same thing every time you stood up against the normal conventions of worldliness to declare God's truth. The world, by nature, does not like holiness, and it will resist anyone who steps out of the crowd to call it to change. And prophets are considered the worst.

But somebody has to do it, and that's why God calls prophets. They do not possess pleasant personalities and are not the "life of the party." They are not swayed by others' opinions, nor would they be considered "nice guys." Nor do they care.

Everything is black or white to them; there are no shades of grey. It is either righteous or it is sin. And for some reason, they feel compelled to tell you so.

Even if you are the king.

You will not find them in the spotlight of a big ministry receiving the crowd's accolades like today's modern prophets. They just don't fit in. The corporate ministries of today are foreign soil to them. They are more suited to wearing camel's hair in the middle of a river than the Brooks Brothers suits and coifed hairdos of this generation's spiritual leaders. And as a result, they walk a lonely path.

Few understand, and even fewer appreciate, and none realize the price.

We think they are made of some kind of steel that doesn't feel the loneliness and the pain of rejection. Since they don't bend to popular attention, we think their hearts are like stones that feel no affinity for others, but the truth is, they are people just like everyone else. They love, they hate, they need, and they feel just like us. They just have to walk a different path and keep on going.

Sometimes, it is for two hundred miles with

no food or water just to hear the voice of God.

I had a dream many years ago of walking in a desert of soft sand, much like the Sahara. Each footstep was difficult as it pushed through the sand. No water, a hot sun, and nothing but sand made it a weariness just to get to the top of the next sand dune and see if the city that I was trying to get to was there. But all that ever appeared was more sand.

I didn't know where I was or if I was heading in the right direction, but I just kept walking, hoping that I wasn't walking in circles. And then I heard a vehicle coming from behind me. A young man with blond hair and a bronze tan drove by in a Dune Buggy, waving to me as he passed by, "Hey, Mr. Garris. I'm off to my ministry! Praise the Lord!." And off he drove over the horizon.

You have to wonder at times like that, what is wrong with me? Why am I here trudging along in this loose desert sand, heading seemingly to nowhere, while this young kid is zooming along so effortlessly into his ministry? What did I do wrong? Will I ever reach that city that I am trying so desperately to find?

Do you ever feel like that? Does it seem so simple for others when everything seems to be a battle for you?

Forty days trudging through the wilderness

just to wait in a cave. Make sense to you? I doubt if it did to Elijah, either. All that way, then climb up a mountain to sit in a cave to wait.

First, the storm, then the earthquake, and then the fire. But still, Elijah waited. And then the still, small voice.

Had Elijah not allowed God to take him through that crucified walk that strips the flesh and breaks the spirit, I don't believe he would have recognized that voice as he did. It would have been just noise, indistinguishable from all the noise of the world.

You may not have to go for two hundred miles without food and water or stand up against a king to declare a spiritual famine upon the land. You may not call down fire from heaven or raise a woman's dead son, but in your soul, you possess the ability to declare the righteousness of God to a worldly church that is mesmerized with an easier, worldly doctrine that mistakes grace for sin and covetousness for prosperity.

You will get the same results as Elijah did, and you will go through the same lonely walk as he walked. But know that you are not alone – there are 7,000 that God had reserved – and you are not walking aimlessly. You will finally step over the hill of that last sand dune and see the City that you've been searching for and you will recognize the still, small voice of God as He speaks to you.

"Well done, my good and faithful servant."

Two Paths Diverged in a Yellow Wood

When I think of the two gospels that I see in America, I sometimes think of that Robert Frost poem, *"Two paths diverged in a yellow wood…"* One gospel is so well accepted that not many people today even know that there is another one. Sure, they've heard of it, but often with criticism and disdain. They are much more enamored with a kinder, gentler gospel that has been tailored for this generation. It is almost universally accepted today as a much more enlightened view of the love of God than those old-fashioned folks who used to preach about fear and hell. They don't even remember anyone who has preached that old gospel.

I must be older than I thought. I'll be 73 in a few weeks, so I guess I am. I still remember that old-time gospel. It was what I got saved with. And it was the message that we saw thousands of others get saved with. Our altars were full every single night and twice on Sundays. People were repenting on their knees in the church, on the phone, on the streets, and over the radio. In ten years, we saw close to 100,000 souls get saved, and it was with that old-fashioned gospel of hell, fire, brimstone, and the fear of God.

It sure seemed like it was working for me, but then, what do I know? Nowadays, these kids have titles, degrees, and fancy diplomas to hang on the wall, certifying that they know stuff. All kinds of stuff. And lots of it, too. I guess eating off the Tree of the Knowledge of Good and Evil can really fill you up because the Bible says that *"knowledge puffeth up."*

Leonard Ravenhill once said that we used to have preachers with no degrees but lots of heat, but now we have preachers with lots of degrees and no heat. I wonder if there is a connection.

Those who pursue ecclesiastical paths rarely see their divergence from the message that their forefathers preached. When they do, they dismiss that old-fashioned gospel as old, caustic, and unnecessarily hard. And yet, you would think that the vast difference in results would give them a clue. The altars of those old-timers were hot and on fire. They won thousands of souls on a continual, daily basis, whereas the altars of this generation are bare and cold with mere handfuls of repentant souls. When we need it the most, we have the least response.

Perhaps our ears are so full of "church" that we can't hear.

"... and knowest not that thou art wretched, and

miserable, and poor, and blind, and naked." (Revelations 3:17)

African Prayer Meetings

> *"And Gideon said unto him, Oh my Lord, if the LORD be with us, why then is all this befallen us? and where be all his miracles which our fathers told us of, saying, Did not the LORD bring us up from Egypt?" Judges 6:13*

As I was standing in front of a small congregation of people, watching them pour up to the altar to get prayed over for healing, I was struck by the look on their faces. I could see hope pouring out from the depths of their souls and the bright expectations of a childlike trust in God. They knew they would be healed and delivered out of the afflictions that had plagued them for who knows how long. The hope was like a bright light that had suddenly pierced into the darkness of their lives, and their expectations were like a newly found energy that gave birth to a burst of inspiration that God had visited them. And there I was, standing in front of them, clueless, scared to death, and wondering, "Oh God, what do I do now?"

The church is in Africa, but my lack of faith was still rooted in America. I don't do miracles. I just preach the Gospel. I don't know how to call up the supernatural, snap my fingers, and bring forth miraculous healings. I don't have any stupid self-help book to rely on like "The 5 Points to Supernatural Healings." It's just me – just me, God, and these desperately needy people. But God healed them anyway – the sick, the lame, the deaf, and the desolate. All of them … in spite of me.

It happens all the time over there. But why do we not see this kind of power exhibited over here in America? Where are the miracles that our forefathers saw a couple of generations ago? Where did God go?

Well, the truth is that there are miracles here. We just don't see them in our modern, sophisticated churches. In my little town alone, I have seen a lady with 4th Stage Cancer healed, a little girl with AIDS healed, a man with Leukemia immediately cured, and many more. I just had breakfast with a man who popped out of a coma just minutes before they were going to pull the plug on him. He was considered medically dead, but God is not constrained by even the threshold of Death. He is only constrained by the lack of serious prayer.

Where is this miraculous manifestation of the power of God in our churches today? Why don't we see this anymore? Something is missing. There is a disconnect between what we read in the Scriptures and what we see in church.

The answer, as usual, came out of the clear, blue sky. Literally.

If God were to pour out His mighty power and bring forth a multitude of unfettered healings in our churches in America today, He would be setting His seal of approval on an apostate church and, by doing so, would be holding them back from the place of broken-hearted repentance that is so desperately needed to restore them to revival. He loves us more than that.

Use whatever reasons you may. Run on with your myriad of worn-out excuses to dismiss this absence of His power, and wax as eloquent as you want with your banal churchy platitudes, but the challenge from Gideon remains unanswered by this generation.

Our prayer meetings for revival are scarce at best — non-existent at worst. And when we do pray, we pray like little girls as we "think" our prayers in our little anemic "quiet time." We hold hands and submit polite requests in low, soothing voices, as if we are afraid to wake anyone up. We are no longer the warriors that called forth the battle that forged our once on-fire churches in the fires of revival. We have become weaklings and have lost our calling as warriors. We just aren't desperate enough to stand up and fight.

Only when we realize how far we have fallen and take on Gideon's refusal to submit to "church as usual" will we ever be able to rise out of our homogenous mediocrity to take up the arms of spiritual war and reclaim the harvest fields that we have allowed the enemy to take from us.

Prayer moves God, but it takes great prayer to see great moves of God. Only when we have determined in our hearts to rock the Throne of God for a great and mighty move will we see Him rise off His Throne and answer.

There is a price to pay for anything from God. When we are finally willing to pay that price, we will have an answer for Gideon.

The Great Danger of Modern Christianity

> *"So that we ourselves glory in you in the churches of God for your patience and faith in all your persecutions and tribulations that ye endure:*
> *Which is a manifest token of the righteous judgment of God, that ye may be counted worthy of the kingdom of God, for which ye also suffer"*
> *(2 Thess. 1:4,5)*

What is Paul saying here? That persecution and tribulation are a sign of the righteous judgment of God? Does that mean that as we declare the righteous judgment of God on a sinful people, we will suffer persecution?

There's another scripture that comes to mind: "Yea, and all that will live godly in Christ Jesus shall suffer persecution." (2 Timothy 3:12)

Am I hearing this right? If you are walking in the Lord the way you are supposed to and declaring the difference between sin and righteousness, then you are going to have trouble. Why? Because people do not want to be told that they have to give up their sin, their pride, and their lusts. The world does not want to hear that there is a burning Hell. They would prefer to gloss over that little detail. And if you remind them of it, they will call you a judgmental legalist who preaches hate and will persecute you as a result.

If you persist, you will find that you won't make many friends.

If you are a pastor, you will find that many of your congregation will leave.

If you're a Christian, what other choice do you have?

If we are easygoing Christians – we make no waves, cause no controversy, never rock the boat or shake up the Church, we're just really nice guys – then, of course, everyone will like us. I can think of a bunch of folks I know that everybody loves. Gosh, they're so much fun to be around, and they always make you feel happy when you're around them. They never get into arguments or heated debates. It seems they would be the epitome of what we should strive to be like. Or is it just that they never take a stand for righteousness?

Avoiding arguments is good. Doctrinal debates can go round and round and never get anywhere, but what about judgment? What about declaring the righteousness of God? Is that just supposed to be a personal matter, or are we supposed to declare that which is right and that which is sin?

This wouldn't be a big deal except for one thing – there's a burning Hell. It Is real and eternal; once you cross into eternity, there is no coming back. That, as they say, is the game-changer. People may not want to hear you tell them about Hell, but what is your responsibility?

Proverbs 24:11,12 tells us,

"If thou forbear to deliver them that are drawn unto death, and those that are ready to be slain; If thou sayest, Behold, we knew it not; doth not he that pondereth the heart consider it? and he that keepeth thy soul, doth not he know it? And shall not he render to every man according to his works?"

This life is not about having fun and enjoying the world, prospering and making money, or attaining stature and fame – it's about escaping the pits of Hell and getting into Heaven.

If that is so, why would you NOT warn people about Hell? Who cares if they don't like it? A confirmed atheist, Penn of the Penn & Teller Vegas show once asked, "If you genuinely believe the Bible, how much hate must you have for someone not to tell them about Hell?

They didn't crucify Christ because He preached Love. They killed Him because He told them to repent.

Then, in the second chapter of 2nd Thessalonians, Paul turns his attention to the Church in the last days. He describes the Antichrist as one who would come in with all kinds of "power, signs and lying wonders" to deceive the Church. This is the same guy that Daniel says would also win the kingdom by flatteries. Which kingdom is that? Could it be the Church? Because after that, he talks about a great falling away and that many would be deceived because *"they received not the love of the truth"* (2nd Thess 2:10), but instead would be damned because they *"believed not the truth, but had pleasure in unrighteousness."* (2nd Thess. 2:12)

It sounds like the Antichrist has the message that people want to hear in contrast to the kind of message that brings persecution. Isaiah tells us that people want to hear "smooth things" instead of the hard truth of righteousness. (Isaiah 30:10). They will believe what they want to believe in spite of the facts and use the Bible to justify themselves. They will then turn to a different gospel that is more to their liking, like that which the Antichrist will give them.

There is a great danger to modern

Christianity, which is averse to judgment and "legalism" but pursues a message of love, grace, and blessings. When we leave those old standard moorings of righteousness, we slide closer and closer to a worldly definition of truth. Feelings become more important than conviction for sin, grace becomes more important than holiness, and being nice is more important than telling the truth.

And what we end up with is a church that can no longer recognize the difference between truth and deception. When people become easily swayed by signs and wonders and begin to run after false prophets to hear the latest "word of blessing from God," they lose the strength to resist the Antichrist's Pied Piper call to a flattering gospel with no conviction, judgment, or righteousness. "…and my people love to have it so" (Jer. 5:31).

As the Church wallows in greater wealth than it has ever known, she becomes flush with the lure of prosperity and material blessings, and it becomes more and more difficult to discern a difference between the Church and the world. Leonard Ravenhill once wrote that there's more of Hollywood than holiness in the church … and that was 20 years ago.

In Judges chapter 6, the Israelites allowed the Amalekites to come in, and in no time, they completely took over and destroyed the harvest. But because the Israelites no longer had a love for the truth, they did not recognize the danger and turned to Baal as the true god. Renegades like Gideon were, therefore, considered wicked and should be killed. The good becomes evil, and the evil becomes good. In like manner, today's church is allowing the world to come in and is falling for a modern gospel and will be easily deceived by the flattery of the Antichrist and the False Prophet.

In 2002, I saw a vision of modern Christianity rushing in a stampede toward the edge of a cliff. As I yelled and tried to warn them, the Lord spoke to me and said, "Even if they could hear you, which they cannot, they will not listen." They were too mesmerized by this new, modern gospel.

> *"Love not the world, neither the things that are in the world. If any man love the world, the love of the Father is not in him." (1 John 2:15)*

Too Tough for Demas

"For Demas hath forsaken me ..." (2 Timothy 4:10)

How must that have felt to this old warrior who had struggled and fought to establish this Gospel that he knew was the only answer to saving the world from Hell. He had fought with demons and deacons, priests and princes. He had endured beatings, mockery, and the threat of prison and death for this cause. He could have been wealthy and powerful, a member of the ruling class in Jerusalem, but he turned it all away because he had met the Nazarene on the road to Damascus.

Paul knew what was at stake – Heaven for those who accepted this new revolutionary doctrine and Hell for those who did not. Jew and Gentile alike faced the utter reality of a devastating judgment. While Peter was given the ministry to the Jews, Paul was handed the enormous task of the rest of the Gentile world. And with that commission was the understanding that salvation would come to the Jews through the Gentiles as they fulfilled their dispensation. He had to succeed; he could not stumble and fail. Too much was hanging in the balance.

And then Demas forsook him.

I don't suppose Paul was a soft-spoken kind of guy. Maybe he was a little too tough on Demas, or maybe he was too intense for him. He had a sharply divided sense of right and wrong and did not mince words to comfort hurt feelings. Rather, he made his points clear and blazingly lucid.

"Reprove, rebuke, exhort with all longsuffering and doctrine." (2 Timothy 4:2)

In other words, tell them the truth! Quit pussyfooting around. Do it in love, but stay true to the doctrine. Why?

"For the time will come when they will not endure sound doctrine: but after their own lusts shall they heap to themselves teachers, having itching ears; and they shall turn away their ears from the truth and shall be turned unto fables." (2Timothy 4:3,4)

I wonder if Paul self-examined himself first when Demas left. "Was I too hard on him? Did I not consider his feelings? Do I have a bad attitude?" These are all questions we ask ourselves when a good friend abandons us.

But at some point, his prophetic spirit had to take back control and say no. Even if his attitude was not socially gracious, the truth is that we are engaged in an insanely ferocious war of eternity. The destiny for billions of souls is at stake.

True love, then, is not the creamy smooth gospel that most people find so alluring. It is the stark and sometimes sharp declaration of truth that cuts away the shrouds of death to liberate the soul to walk in true righteousness in the fear of God – a doctrine that is often not the favored choice of many.

Somebody has to take that stand. Paul did. Demas did not.

Dissolving Hymenaeus

> *"Now the end of the commandment is charity out of a pure heart, and of a good conscience, and of faith unfeigned: From which some having swerved have turned aside unto vain jangling; Desiring to be teachers of the law; understanding neither what they say, nor whereof they affirm."*
> *"Of whom is Hymenaeus and Alexander…"* 1st Timothy 1:5-7,20

I don't ever want to be one of those guys that your pastor warns you about. They're right there in church in the midst of everyone, and they think they are so right that they have to make sure everyone knows it. But they're not. And they don't know it.

Imagine being someone like that. You know there is a separation between you and everyone else, especially the church leadership, and yet you excuse it by thinking that it is because you are just a little better than them. After all, you know you're right, but most people just don't understand. After all, the Bible does say in Proverbs that they that seek the Lord understand all things. That must explain why others just don't get it, and you do. What a trap of delusion! And how easy it is to fall into it!

What a surprise awaits them. All the way up to their last breath, they think they are so right with God, and then their reality crashes down on them in an instant. The sad thing is that their time of boasting is so fleeting, but their judgment is forever.

I don't want to be one of those guys, so how do I make sure that I do not fall into that trap? I can only think of three things:

1. Focus on others.
   One of the principles of revival that I preach is that the Gospel is not about you; it is about others. Throughout the Bible, the Lord directs our focus to others, others, others. I always say that if you don't get this, you will never understand the Cross, because that is the central reason why He came, and He tells us to do the same (Matt. 16:24)
   Forget about yourself and focus on others. It will dissolve your pride and arrogance like hot water on butter.

2. You don't always have to be right.
   Let others have their opinion and perspective. It's okay. You don't have to take on the role of the Lord High Executioner or the Holy and Exalted Fruit Inspector. For crying out loud, let

it go! Relax. You don't have to correct all the world's mistakes.

3. You aren't always right.
   Yeah, this goes with #2. Maybe, just maybe, you aren't always right. Did that ever occur to you? You might even learn something if you kept your mouth shut. Maybe you'd learn that not only you are not what you think you are, but that it doesn't matter anyway. This is not a matter of who gets the highest score at the Judgment Bar or how much "stuff" you know. Let me tell you, nobody cares. Especially not God. So, who are you trying to impress?

And that is probably the heart of the issue. People like that have a weakness somewhere inside them that Satan has exploited and that they are trying to compensate for. What is it that they are trying to prove? Maybe they don't really think they're better; maybe they're just afraid they're not.

However, the heart of this issue is not just about us not falling into that trap but of us having mercy by praying for those who have. (See #1).

After all, that is the whole point, isn't it?

Evidence

"And his disciples asked him, saying, Why then say the scribes that Elias must first come?

And Jesus answered and said unto them, Elias truly shall first come, and restore all things. But I say unto you, That Elias is come already, and they knew him not, but have done unto him whatsoever they listed. Likewise, shall also the Son of man suffer of them. Then the disciples understood that he spake unto them of John the Baptist." (Matthew 17:10-13)

They had just come down from the mountain - Peter, James, and John. They got to see what no one else had ever seen nor would see. They saw Jesus in His glory. Plus, they saw Moses and Elijah! Are you kidding? They were there! They could have reached out and touched them!

Not only that, but the most unbelievable thing that could ever happen had just happened to them - they heard God the Father speak. And He spoke to them, directly, personally!

Who are you going to tell? Who is going to believe that God the Father actually spoke directly to you? The other disciples all believed in Jesus as the Christ, but c'mon, Peter, aren't you stretching things a little? Who do you guys think you are? Oh sure, you saw Moses, and he was having a chat with Elijah. Uh-huh.

And forget about telling anyone on the outside. They're having a tough enough time deciding whether or not Jesus is the Messiah that should come or just another crazy false prophet. The Lord knows they had enough of them, especially during that particular time. If they went out telling everyone what they had just seen, people would think they were crazy.

So, who do you tell? And yet, they knew that they had seen this incredible thing.

But now they are struggling with how to answer the Pharisees and the gainsayers, the doubting clergy who thought they knew so much more than these stupid, uneducated fishermen. The Scripture plainly says that Elias must precede the Messiah. It's right there in Malachi. Look around you. Where's Elijah? We don't see anybody coming down riding his chariot of fire, and it's sure not one of you guys. So where is he? And — the follow up to that — if there is no Elijah here, then Jesus cannot be the Christ.

And yet they knew. They saw with their own

eyes. They heard the voice of God. But how do you answer this?

There are times when you don't know what to say, but you have that gut feeling, a confidence of faith, that you know that you know that it is true. You may not have the answer, and you have nothing to counter your critics with, but you know it is true.

There will be times like that when you can feel Satan laughing in your face because it looks like you have lost the argument. But as they say, he who laughs last laughs best of all. Hang onto the solid substance of faith you have anchored in your heart and declare your faith, for you are NOT wrong, even though you may not know the answer. Declare your victory no matter what, for we are saved by faith, not by sight!

Oh, and as for Elijah? That's easy. It was John the Baptist. Any other questions?

"Now faith is the substance of things hoped for, the evidence of things not seen." (Hebrews 11:1)

Hope

Oh God, where are you? Can you see me? Are you watching? Or are you busy paying attention to 7 billion other people who need you just as much or more than I do?

Have You chosen to set yourself apart from us, just far enough back so that we can almost touch You, but not so close that it would dissolve faith? Sometimes, there are miracles; sometimes, all the crying in the world cannot get You to move. Sometimes, I can feel the Spirit so strong I feel like dancing; sometimes, it feels like the heavens are brass and the door to Your presence is slammed shut. Sometimes, You feel so close that I feel enveloped in you; sometimes, You are so far away that I wonder if You are really there or not.

Belief in God has never been natural for me. The whole concept of God watching over us seemed so foreign to me that it was much easier to believe in the postulates of science than in the hopes of Heaven. Why would God do things this way? How come He doesn't show Himself in the sky so we can all settle this debate once and for all? He does, after all, want everybody to go to Heaven, right? So where exactly is He?

And really, where is Heaven? Is it some far-out place way out in the cosmos or buried in some other dimension? How come it is way out there, and we are down here?

We are immersed in the reality of this tangible world, and it, therefore, captures our attention. Sometimes, it's a lot easier to <u>not</u> believe than to believe, especially when you're praying your guts out, and it seems like God is deaf. Heaven can only be hoped for, not seen.

But then there are those times when God reaches down and touches you. Or heals some blind person. Or answers some prayer of yours that was just impossible. Or reaches out and touches you in a place way down in your heart that even you didn't know was there.

Sometimes, He just acts like God, and it is unmistakably Him. And then you know.

Saving Nineveh

"Then Jonah prayed unto the Lord his God out of the fish's belly ..." (Jonah 2:1)

I imagine it was a bright, sunny day - blue skies, birds singing, and a gentle breeze blowing in from the sea. It must have been a beautiful day. At least it was for Jonah. After three days of hell, he had finally been delivered out of the belly of that whale. He might have been slimy and acid-eaten, but he was standing on dry ground ... alive! Yes, it must have been a beautiful day.

But this ordeal wasn't about Jonah. The survival of 120,000 people was depending on this. I'm not sure if Jonah did not want God to deliver the Assyrians, or if he was just plain scared to walk into the midst of these fierce, merciless people and tell them they were going to hell. The point is, he didn't want to go.

But God did.

Acts of mercy that we perform are generated, not from our own wells of charity, but from the heart of God. He just allows us to participate. And it is prayer that unlocks the door to that mercy.

It may be hard for us to believe that our tiny prayers could move continents and drop mountains into the sea, but are we limiting God or ourselves? James 5:16 says that the effectual fervent prayer of a righteous man avails much. Much – as in, a lot, because prayer unties the hands of God so that our works of faith become His works of action. True, there are conditions that God requires for effective prayer, but there are no limitations. If you can imagine it, God can do it.

Prayer is an act of mercy. Mercy, even unintended, is still mercy. We may be praying for something entirely different – Jonah was certainly not praying for the Ninevites – but the effects of prayer, like the random twists and turns of a stream on its way to the sea, can often take circuitous routes to reach God's intended purpose. We are just required to pray. And prayer moves God. And it may not be in the way you intended.

The works of faith can move mountains. They may not be the mountains you were concerned about, but sometimes God puts you into a situation where you have to pray your heart out, often for your own deliverance, just so He can work through your prayers to bring about unintended consequences and move in ways that you could not have imagined.

Including saving 120,000 people who you

never intended to save.

The Effectiveness of Charles Spurgeon

Revivals have to be prayed in. I think just about everyone agrees; I just don't think most people comprehend what that really means.

It has been said that Charles Spurgeon was one of the greatest revival preachers, but he, on his own account, attributed everything to his church. According to David Smithers in a wonderful article about Spurgeon, when visitors would come, he would take them to the basement of his church and show them the people on their knees contending before God for souls and declare that this was the powerhouse of the church. "In Spurgeon's eyes, the prayer meeting was the most important meeting of the week." It was this furnace room, not his preaching, that brought the great moves of God that came through him.

Search through revival history, and you will find the same intense reliance on prayer for any move of God. Prior to any serious revival or move of God, people will be crying out to God, sometimes for years before the heavens break wide open. This is the labor room of travail for the Bride of Christ to give birth to revival. Only this kind of intense passion, tears, and travail will move God into a ferocious outpouring of the Holy Spirit.

The Book of Joel, God's blueprint for revival, cries to us to bring the entire church into the prayer meeting – including the babies – and cry out to God all night long until He answers. This is what God has laid out for us to do if we want revival. There are no shortcuts, no special circumstances, and no alternate methods.

Okay, so we all know this. We've all heard it a thousand times. Yup, we need to pray. Yup, yup, yup. So, when are we going to do it? Excuse me, but we know this is correct, right? So, what will it take to crank up the fire? How do we stir up the hearts of the Church to rise up in faith, expectation, and zeal to charge into the prayer room to tear down every principality that stands in the way and shake the Throne of God for the supernatural?

Good question. I wish I had a good answer. If people are not genuinely charged up in the Holy Spirit, their guilty feelings and manufactured zeal will only take them so far. They know they should do this, but their hearts are dragging far behind. As I have said before, water seeks its own level, and it won't take long before people settle back down to their "comfort spot." How do we raise the level of that water and crank up the fire in people's hearts?

I asked the Lord that question. His answer was simple. Do you want to raise the level of the water? Then add more water. Hmmmm.

Water throughout the Bible represents the Word of God. The point is simple. We can't turn ourselves into instant prayer warriors through our own efforts. Go ahead. Try it. Pray for 3 hours a day in a strong, loud, contending voice as Elijah did. Let me know how far you get. Only God can give you the power to pray like that. And where does that power come from? The Word. Prayer without faith is pointless; faith comes by hearing and hearing by the Word of God.

This is not exactly a slam dunk, and there is not enough space here to go into a long dissertation on the mechanics of the formulation of revival, but suffice it to say that devouring the Word of God is a good place to start. Without me, Jesus said, you can do nothing … and He WAS the Word of God.

The rest depends on those faithful few who, in receiving their power and faith from the Word of God, know how to contend in prayer and have been battle-trained in storming the Throne of God. This is not for the polite silent prayers of well-meaning church people who clasp their hands and silently offer their thoughts, but for those outrageous souls who will stop at nothing to make their voices heard from on High. This is war, not a skirmish, and the price for failure is not death, but eternal torment for countless millions of souls if you do not succeed.

When we look at the great revival preachers that God has used in the past, let us not make the mistake of thinking that they were responsible for the revivals that God brought through them. No, it came through the desperate prayers of some few dedicated faithful saints who refused to accept defeat, but claimed, fought, and won the victory with broken hearts, tear-laden cries, and bended knees in that prayer room … and who hung on to the horns of the altar until God moved.

You want revival? Then somebody has to get down on their knees.

Battleground

"I will therefore that men pray everywhere..."
1 Timothy 2:8

It has been said that preaching moves men, but prayer moves God. If that is the case, then it seems to me that we should do a lot more praying than preaching and a lot more time on our knees listening to God than sitting on our butts reading books. Why is it that prayer seems to be the most neglected of all Christian duties?

The secret art of prayer intercession has become rare because it taxes the depths of your soul to contend before the Throne of God for hours in an all-out struggle to wage war. Few Christians care enough to pray that much. It is much easier to fellowship with other Christians than to lock oneself in that solitary closet for hours in travail with God. That secret place of the Most High is not for the light and easy Christian who is content with Sunday services and professes a relatively clean life but shrinks from crossing over to a crucified, broken walk of sacrifice. They nibble at the Word of God and sip at the fountain of prayer, so they never receive the strength to break through to a deeper level in God. They "have a little talk with Jesus" but never grapple with contending prayer. Is it a small wonder that we have more faith in our carnal efforts than in a supernatural answer to prayer?

The prayer room is the battleground of Eternity. It is there that all battles are fought and won ... or lost through the weakness of the flesh. This is where we serve the Lord. Before anything can be accomplished on the streets, in the pulpit, or in any human endeavor, the victory must first be established in prayer. Anything short of that would be stealing the glory from God because if <u>we</u> accomplish it, then we can take the credit, but prayer – deep prevailing prayer – hands the victory over to God. Attempting to serve God without being saturated with prayer until we have the victory in hand leads to spiritual pride and holiness of the flesh. We think we are doing great things by serving the Lord in the flesh, but all we are accomplishing is bolstering our own self-righteousness.

There are two things this generation seems to have lost. One is the ability to pray something all the way through until we receive an answer from God — not a wisp of our imagination, but a real supernatural breakthrough. Instead, we have convinced ourselves that we can make do with a time limit for our requests. As a result, we resort to wishful thinking instead of faith to guide our Christian lives.

The other thing we seem to have forgotten is the ability to pray like a warrior. I hear people proudly mention their "quiet time" with God each morning. I believe them. Nobody's talking, and nobody's answering. Is this how Elijah stopped the rain? Could it be that this is the reason our generation has no miracles, no outpouring in our services, no supernatural moves of God, and no souls at the altar getting saved?

Maybe God isn't answering us because He can't hear us.

The Theology of Prayer

"When we become too glib in prayer, we are most surely talking to ourselves." - A. W. Tozer

Passionless prayer is not what Paul referred to when he wrote about striving in prayer. The word he used was "*agonizomai*," which means to struggle in a wrestling match, not just to finish, but to win against all odds.

Is your prayer hour like that, or is it just "a little talk with Jesus"? Is your prayer time described as contending with God like Jacob or Elijah, or is it your "quiet time with Jesus"?

A.W. Tozer knew what he was saying would ruffle some feathers because people without passion will almost always choose comfort over contending. But he said it anyway because it is true.

There is no substitute for contending prayer. I was taught early on that when you have a problem, take it to the prayer room and seek the face of God. Keep praying until you get an answer - fast if you have to -- but get your answers from God. If you don't understand something, give it to God, and when you are ready to receive the answer, He will give it to you.

But this generation has instead made a habit of seeking Christian self-help books for answers to their spiritual problems. They read book after book, seeking answers, and then they will check with the Bible to see if it lines up with what they have chosen to believe. They are substituting reading books for prayer.

I can hear all the voices rising up to tell me about all the wonderful things they've learned from books. I would answer that, besides missing a personal experience from your Father, the real problem is that you don't know if they are right or wrong. Maybe they're mostly right ... like 99% right. And we all know that 1% is the pebble in the stream that nudges your direction just a little bit off the true course, setting you up for the next pebble and the next until the stream ends up in a very different destination.

Am I too old-fashioned? Maybe. But I'd rather get my answers from God because He is always right. *"Call unto me, and I will answer thee, and shew thee great and mighty things, which thou knowest not." (Jeremiah 33:3)*

Agonizomai

> "*I am rich, and increased with goods, and have need of nothing...*" Revelations 3:17

Prevailing prayer is an acquired taste. It is not something that is flipped on with a switch or developed with a snap of the fingers. And once acquired, it can be all too easy to lose because the very nature of prevailing prayer demands an intensity that is born out of desperation – something that our flesh does not possess in and of itself.

When I consider the Church in America, I see a structure that has been built to great heights but is, nevertheless, only a shell of what those who built it had intended for it to be. Whatever happened to the great warriors of the Faith that we have read about? There are plenty of books written about the great exploits and power of these men and women of God who tore down strongholds, established a Gospel of power in the land, and changed the very fabric of our society. But today, we have nice pastors preaching nice messages to very nice people in large, comfortable, nice churches.

Am I missing something here? When did we get so comfortable?

When we were first saved, how thrilled we were to be ushered into our new relationship with God! The curtain of Eternity had parted for us, and we could touch the Throne of God and commune with Almighty God. I had never experienced anything like that in my life. None of us had. And so, we prayed with a fervor and intensity that pierced the heavens and ignited a fire within us that drove us even further into the Spirit of God. We were on fire for God!

As life progressed, however, and we settled into a more normal routine in life – house, car, job, kids – our intensity began to fade. We still considered ourselves good, established Christians – we never missed church, lived clean lives, professed our Christianity, and were never ashamed of our faith – but somehow, that wild, exciting fire that used to burn inside us had settled down. Perhaps we were no longer as desperate as we once were. Maybe we just got used to being saved, or maybe we just didn't feel the need. Whatever it was, our ardor cooled down, and we became the very ones we had once disdained as lukewarm.

The problem is that we never saw it coming and cannot see it in ourselves today. Ask any one of us, and we will be quick to tell you what on-fire Christians we are: true and faithful, strong and sharp. But there are no fruits of our labor that we can point to. Oh, we are active in all sorts of church activities, but how many souls have we won? Well, uh, we support all kinds of works and help out wherever we can ... sort of.

And then there are those who are so holy that they refuse to go to church because they don't want to be tainted by those whom they have deigned as lukewarm. They refuse to be associated with a "dead church," so they recuse themselves from any responsibility to the Body of Christ. They shrink back into their cave of self-righteousness where they can peer through the opening of the cave at the rest of us poor Christians who hold a dimmer light than themselves. And where is the fruit of their labor? How far abroad has the love of God been spread by their testimony? Not much farther than the opening of their self-appointed prison.

I can understand each perspective, and I can relate to how easy it is to slide into a quiet mediocrity or ascetic reclusiveness. At one point in time or another, I have experienced the same, but any of those positions could still be justified if they were backed up by strong, agonizing prayer for revival, for souls, and for the kingdom of God. But that's the problem ... they're not.

I never hear about the victorious battles these

people have waged in the prayer room, or what a strong prayer hour they have had recently, or how they had a great all-night prayer meeting and saw the light of victory in the early morning hours. It makes me wonder if they even know what it means to pray like that ... or are they so absorbed with their own righteousness that they have not considered the plight of others and the essence of the call of the Cross?

Maybe I'm the one who is being judgmental or critical here. Maybe I just don't see the glow of their spiritual life that is hidden inside somewhere. But if that is the case, where is the manifestation of the power of God? Where are the fruits? Where are souls getting saved? If there is a fire burning inside you, why can't I smell the smoke?

The funny thing is that the same things that are true about us also perfectly describe our churches today. I guess you could say that we are what we eat.

I believe it all goes back to the prayer room. The Christian you are on your knees is the Christian you will be out in the world. When there is no fire burning in the furnace room, there will be no heat in you or in your church, and the results of a cold faith will show up at your empty altars.

There is a Greek word that Paul used to describe how we should walk as Christians –

agonizomai. It means to struggle and wrestle as in a contest or game, making every effort to win the victory. It is to contend in a task of faith by persevering amid temptation and oppression, and it means to strive and labor fervently in special pains and toil until you have won. He uses it to describe prayer.

Do we agonize in prayer like our forefathers did? It was their agonizomai that laid the foundation of faith to win our souls. Are we doing the same for others? I have to believe that if we were, God would answer. And if he does not, what does that say about our faith?

If there was a fire burning in us, you could smell the smoke and feel the heat. But our altars are barren, cold brass because the fire has gone out. The horns on those altars are no longer covered with blood. We go through our religious ceremonies of "church as usual," but there is no incense going up before the Throne, no sacrifices of blood, and as a result, there is no move of God in our land.

"And I looked, and there was none to help; and I wondered that there was none to uphold: therefore mine own arm brought salvation unto me; and my fury, it upheld me." (Isa 63:5)

Releasing Praise

> *"Then took Mary a pound of ointment of spikenard, very costly, and anointed the feet of Jesus, and wiped his feet with her hair: and the house was filled with the odor of the ointment."*
> *(John 12:3)*

Praise contradicts pride. If you are praising God, He becomes your focus, not yourself. The fragrance fills the room, and the presence of this world and its hold on you is squeezed out. Pride melts away along with your attention on yourself. You – your position, your title, your benefit and welfare, your prosperity and blessings, even your place in God – dissolve in the cloud of unfettered praise carried in the beauty of holiness.

Pride is nothing more than putting yourself above everyone else, including God. It has a ravenous appetite and will take over every place it enters. Just as the flesh wars against the Spirit, so pride is the antithesis of praise, and just as sin separates us from God, so also is grace unable to function in the presence of pride.

If you do not let go of your pride, your praises

to God will ring hollow, and it will not be long before you are bored with repeating the meaningless phrases of "praise you, Jesus, thank you, Jesus." The flesh takes precedent over lifeless words and renders your praises impotent. Your connection to the Holy Spirit is then broken and your feet remain planted in this world.

How, then, do we anchor our praises in the Spirit, break the stranglehold of the flesh, and release true praise and worship? The answer, as always, is to immerse yourself in the Word. All power comes from the Word of God. The Word of God created the universe. It cleanses you, gives you light and understanding, and because it is the source of faith, it gives you the power to pray. And prayer is the key that opens the door to praise.

There is one more step, however, in releasing the full power of praise. You have to break your heart. Mary broke the alabaster box that held the ointment. In so doing, you break open the bars that hold praise captive and liberate it to fill the room.

The power of praise is one of the secrets to answered prayer. You *"enter His courts with praise"* (Psalms 100:4). Praise opens the door to the Throne Room of God. When you are immersed in praise and worship, the Holy Spirit will cover you and carry you into the presence of God. Once you are standing before Him in all His glory, nothing else matters.

Turn your eyes upon Jesus,
Look full in His wonderful face,
And the things of earth will grow strangely dim,
In the light of His glory and grace.

(Helen H. Lemel)

Trust in God

Your trust in God is dependent upon your prayer life.

In today's religious environment, we hear all about how we should trust God. Don't worry about anything because God will take care of you. He loves you and will not let anything bad happen to you. I'm sorry, but that is neither faith nor trust. That's presumption.

Just because you say something or make some "prophetic" proclamation does not necessarily mean it is true or will happen. But I often hear supposedly real Christians quote the passage in Romans 4:17, *"…before him whom he believed, even God, who quickeneth the dead, and calleth those things which be not as though they were" and* use it to claim that we can call things into creation or that just because we proclaim it, it has to happen.

Where did we get that from? That statement applies to God and God only. It does not give you the power to "Name it and Claim it." Neither does it bequeath unto you power to make anything happen. Accessing power through the words that you speak is not faith. It is sorcery.

1st Corinthians 4:20 tells us that the kingdom of God is NOT in word, but in power. Power in God – real power – does not come with the snap of your fingers. It is earned slowly, the hard way. It comes from hours on your knees in deep, prevailing prayer. Your little "quiet time with Jesus" will not break through the holy of holies to pierce the heavens. Matthew 11:12 says that the violent take the kingdom of heaven by force. Is that how you pray? Is your prayer room a place of battle, a contending before the Throne of God, and a place of violent spiritual warfare?

Crucifying your flesh through fasting and prayer breaks your fleshly desires and paves the way into the presence of God. The flesh lusts against the Spirit and the Spirit against the flesh. (Gal. 5:17). We cannot get to a place of real power in God if we are still walking in uncrucified flesh. We have to break through ourselves first before we can see breakthroughs in our walk in God.

Everybody wants to be a prophet, but nobody wants to pay the price. They think it's as easy as "speaking the word." Just click your heels together three times, hold a good thought, speak a word of prophecy, and BINGO! Just like that, we are in the Land of Oz!

We have lost the fear of God that should have

kept us back from such foolish sin. Prophets of peace and prosperity abound because we love to hear fake prophesies about our prosperity and blessings, but real prophets of God who are called to bring us to repentance, (Jer. 23:22) are rejected as being too judgmental, hard, caustic, and legalistic. So, we heap up to ourselves teachers that tell us what our itching ears want to hear (2 Tim. 4:3). But God says that because we did not love the truth, He would turn us over to believe a lie (2Thess. 2:10-12)

To fully trust God, you must find your place in Him – that secret place of the Most High (Psalm 91:1) – and when you have touched the Throne of God, you know that you know that you know that you have solid confidence that your trust in God is not based on wishful thinking or presumptuous flesh, but upon your communion with God Himself.

You get your trust in Him when you touch the Throne of God.

Touch Not My Anointed

Touch not mine anointed, and do my prophets no harm. (Psalms 105:15)

I think it is no secret that Satan would try anything to destroy the Church. To keep the flock from straying under Satan's influence, the Lord has placed the church under the authority of the pastor. Deacons and elders play a subordinate role in most churches, and we are supposed to be subject to one another, but the truth is, most often, the pastor is fully in charge, and the flock is supposed to submit to him.

But who does the pastor answer to?

I have heard Benny Hinn say that we should not reprove the pastors because we are not to "touch His anointed," using David and Saul as the example. Let me remind you that while David would not come against Saul, Samuel had no such inhibition, nor did Nathan, Micaiah, Amos, or any other prophet of God. The king may be in charge, but by God, he'd better listen to the prophet!

That scripture, however, has nothing to do with the reproof of a pastor. It is about protection from the enemy. David is speaking in Psalms 105 about how God protected Abraham, Isaac, and Jacob from those who would come against them. He was not talking about reproving pastors and holding them accountable.

So, who holds our pastors in check or guides them when they stray? That is the job of a prophet.

A true prophet has a solitary walk. In order to be able to reprove kings, his message cannot be influenced by anyone. He must remain separate, consecrated unto God alone. His job is to stand in the gaps (Eze. 13:5) and call the church, and most especially the leadership, back to a place of repentance. He is not called to be popular or make friends. Jesus said that no prophet is honored in his own country and among his own people. Why? Because he doesn't tell them what they want to hear. When you do see a prophet that is honored in his own country, it is most likely because he is a prophet of "peace and prosperity."

Modern prophets of peace and prosperity in this generation like to lean heavily on the scripture in 1st Corinthians 14:3 in their effort to "speak unto us smooth things" (Isa. 30:10), but they never call us to repentance. According to Jeremiah, however, that call to bring the church to a place of repentance is the litmus test of a true prophet of God (Jer. 23:22), a test that many of today's blessing prophets fail.

Prophets are called, as in chapter 14 of Leviticus, to scour and cut out leprosy in the house. If the leprosy is cured, then the house can remain. If it is not, then the entire house and everything left in it are to be burned outside the camp. When the leadership of any church will not allow itself to be reproved, leprosy will grow unabated in that house. Satan is ecstatic because he can continue to lead the pastor away without the terrible interference from God's prophet. It is now only a matter of time before that church falls.

The real losers in this are the unsaved. Sinners will not flock to altars that have lost their anointing.

And that was Satan's goal all along.

"And he said, I have been very jealous for the LORD God of hosts: for the children of Israel have forsaken thy covenant, thrown down thine altars, and slain thy prophets with the sword; and I, even I only, am left; and they seek my life, to take it away." (1Kings 19:10)

Gratitude on the Beach

Then Jonah prayed unto the LORD his God out of the fish's belly, ²And said, I cried by reason of mine affliction unto the LORD, and he heard me; out of the belly of hell cried I, and thou heardest my voice.

For thou hadst cast me into the deep, in the midst of the seas; and the floods compassed me about: all thy billows and thy waves passed over me.
Then I said, I am cast out of thy sight; yet I will look again toward thy holy temple.
(Jonah 2:1-4)

He could hear the waves crashing behind him, sweeping the water up the sand, never quite coming close to his feet. The whale lay there half in and half out of the water, its life running out of it with every last wheezing breath. Jonah was alone on the beach. He was alive, but more than that, God had heard him down in the whale's belly and had brought him forth into the daylight that he had almost despaired of seeing again.

But here he was, standing alone on the beach

on dry land, next to this great, dying body of a fish that had committed suicide to bring him here. God had delivered him so completely that he hadn't even gotten his feet wet. And now it was time for the mission that he had run away from not even a week ago.

Jonah is not a classic example of gratitude. Jonah cared more about himself than the salvation of 120,000 people. He went ahead and prophesied to the Ninevites as he was commanded to do, but his heart wasn't in it. He was more grateful for a tree that gave him shade than the great deliverance God had done for those people.

Why is that? As a young Christian, I was taught that if you had a thankful heart, you would never backslide, and I have seen the truth of that over the years, but how does one develop a thankful heart?

I don't believe gratitude comes from the things that have happened to you as much as it does from a thankful heart that has already been planted within you. Gratitude is more the blossoming of an attitude you already have rather than the genesis of a new one that you have tried to manufacture. And I believe it is tied to Charity.

One of the six principles of revival that I preach about is that the gospel is not about you; it is about others. This is the central message of the Cross; it is the essence of who and what Christ was. Charity is the essential element, not only to entering into a vibrant and deep walk in God, but to seeing the power of God work in your life. Charity is Jesus Christ working in you.

You would think that gratitude would be about what happens to us rather than to others, but the seeds of gratitude cannot find a place to grow in the stony rock of a cold heart. They can only find purchase in the cultivated soil of a heart that is not only thankful but is softened with that which turns our focus onto others, dismisses our own situation, and rejoices in what God has done for all.

Gratitude is tied to the Cross.

Charity suffereth long, and is kind; charity envieth not; charity vaunteth not itself, is not puffed up,

Doth not behave itself unseemly, seeketh not her own, is not easily provoked, thinketh no evil;

Rejoiceth not in iniquity, but rejoiceth in the truth;

Beareth all things, believeth all things, hopeth all things, endureth all things.

Charity never faileth … (1 Cor. 13: 4-8)

The Garments of Humility

Humility is not something that can be earned, learned, or absorbed. You have to be broken to obtain it.

I've listened to many who try to wear some ill-fitting garments of humility, but they just don't seem to fit correctly. Oh, they sound like they are so humble, but it almost comes across as an excuse rather than something real. While they deprecate themselves to others, it sounds more like an attachment to cover up something that is trying to stick up through their clothing.

The garment of humility is made from the same cloth as the mantle of authority in God. Fake humility, on the other hand, has to refuse the mantle of true authority because it is not the same garment that they are trying to fit into. If one professes to be "oh so humble," where will he get the holy boldness to stand up to take power and dominion over the works of darkness? They don't fit together.

Pride, whether it manifests itself in arrogance or fake humility, is a result of measuring oneself up against those around you. When Saul was little in his own eyes, he hid in "the stuff" because he was afraid to become king. Two years later, he disdained the commandments of the Lord's prophet and decided to offer his own sacrifice to God.

Humility, however, does not measure itself against others but against the Almighty God. With David, it was never about himself – it was always about God. That enabled him to slay Goliath in his youth and rule as king in his old age.

When God calls a servant to manifest His power, there is a cycle that he must go through. When the first miracles begin to flow through a person, it feels like the coolest thing that has ever happened to you. You are so excited that you can't wait to tell others of the wonderful works of God. As you go on, however, a little voice starts to whisper in your ear suggesting that, yes, God did this miracle, but He chose you to do it. Sure, God could have chosen anyone, but hey, He chose you. That must mean you're just a little bit special, doesn't it?

And then it stops — What happened? — and the soul-searching begins.

When you allow God to sand you down to bare metal and let you see your own foolish pride, you make it possible for Him to take you to the next level. And so goes the building process: paint a layer, sand it down, paint a layer, sand it down. There is no one so holy and great that does not have to go through this process. You must be broken to go to the next level because God will not share His glory with anyone.

Only after you have been broken so many times that your ego has been completely burned out of you and your soul has surrendered and yielded to total subjection can you ever be allowed to walk in real power. It is in the luster of that many-layered finish that true humility begins to shine with a light that does not come from you but is reflected from the glory of God.

It is at this point that warriors are brought forth shouldering the mantle of God's anointing and His authority – a mantle, not resplendent with the glory of shining armor, but with the dull luster of sackcloth and ashes.

Calvinism and the Issue of Blood

"And, behold, a woman, which was diseased with an issue of blood twelve years, came behind him, and touched the hem of his garment: For she said within herself, If I may but touch his garment, I shall be whole." Matthew 9:19

There is something about the doctrine of predestination that goes against the grain. Its proponents are quick to point out their usual levy of scriptures and then shrug their shoulders as they hold up their hands with the inevitable reproof that this is just simply the way it is, that God is sovereign and can do whatever He pleases.

Yeah, I suppose that's true, but somehow it just doesn't fit the personality of God as it is written in the "volume of the Book." And when something doesn't fit, you usually have the wrong jigsaw piece in the wrong spot. Yes, you can cram it in there, like forcing a round peg into a square hole, but it never truly fits, and you're never completely comfortable with it. Or, to quote James 3:17, it's not "easy to be entreated."

Could it be that John Calvin got himself an

idea and wrapped his ensuing theology around it, hammering it tight with some of the nails he found scattered throughout the Word of God? Could it be that just maybe there's something more than what is apparent on the surface, a deeper dimension, shall we say, that encompasses a grander vision of God?

Physicists grapple with two realities that are both mathematically sound, and yet refuse to work together in synchronization. Both Newtonian and Quantum physics are correct, and both contradict the other. We know there has to be something more that will give us a great unifying theory. We just don't know what it is.

Not so with theology! There seems to be a compulsion to prove that we are right, as it was with Mr. Calvin.

Calvinism states that no matter what you do, you have no say over whether God will pick you for Heaven or Hell. That sounds suspiciously like Islam. Only those who die in jihad can be sure that they will get to Heaven and get the 70 virgins. Good luck with hoping they are not some toothless old hags plucked from the Ganges River. The rest of the Muslim world has to hope Allah capriciously chooses to let them in. That's called Election, and it is the same for Calvin as it is for Mohammed.

Let me ask you this, if the doctrine of

predestination is correct and you cannot change your election, why did Jesus speak in parables?

I believe in the utterly miraculous gift of free will. I believe it is so far beyond carnal understanding that we can only grasp it by faith. I may not have all the answers, but I do have a grip on the substance of faith, that Jesus Christ died for my sins, and it is my choice to follow Him or reject that Grace. While I could fence with a raft of scriptures to prove my theological point, I refuse to argue. I just believe. And that is what we are asked to do – take it by faith because you can never figure it all out.

Calvin tried his best to untie a spiritual Gordian knot and just got tangled up in the process. I, on the other hand, prefer to throw my lot in with the simple woman with the issue of blood who believed.

But Jesus turned him about, and when he saw her, he said, Daughter, be of good comfort; thy faith hath made thee whole. (Matthew 9:20)

Blood, Fire, Fear, and Souls of Men

There are four indicators that, although not conclusive or all-embracing, show the depth of a ministry. Those are Blood, Fire, Fear, and Souls of men. These may not embody the total essence of Christianity, but without these elements, a ministry shows a lack of wisdom, understanding, and authority in God.

When you're wondering what's missing regarding power, depth, and strength in a particular ministry, look to see if these elements are present. You will often find that when a church emphasizes other things instead of these essentials, as good as those other things may be, that ministry will seem to be running out of gas. Their candle is flickering, their oil is about to run out, and they are sliding into the same category of "church" that the old prophets clamored against. They may be comfortable as far as their stand in the community goes, but if I may so say, there is no comfort in being lukewarm.

Let me explain, one at a time, what I mean by these four elements:

Blood: When there is not a strong

pronouncement in actual words of "the Blood of Jesus," there is a lack of spiritual understanding, not only of the power that is in that Blood but also of the powers of darkness. Satan cannot stand even the mention of the Blood of Jesus. It is a prime weapon in our warfare. I have heard and read Sinners' Prayers that don't mention being washed in that Blood, and I have been in services where it has not ever been mentioned. Have we forgotten that it was only by the Blood of Jesus that redemption was won? Victory was won through the Blood of Jesus Christ. That is the very thing that defeated Satan once and for all. It is the one thing that he cannot stand against.

It has been said that if you know God, you will know the devil, and, if you don't know the devil, you don't know God. Never underestimate the enemy. We are in a fierce war, and if we are not aware of it at all times, we will be seduced into a deadly slumber. For us to gain complete and total victory over sin, we have to remain covered in that Blood. We may hear the words "the Blood of Jesus" in our churches, but what we need is to emphasize the dramatic importance of the power of those words. Remember, we are in enemy territory, and he thinks we're trespassing.

Fire: When I speak of fire, not only am I referring to the lack of fire in our souls, but the lack of an emphasis on a true picture of Hell. Hell is a real place—a terrible place. We didn't create it, but it is most definitely there. Why do we then try to smooth it over with expressions like "Christless eternity" or "separation from God" and other such socially acceptable phases?

Consider for a moment that Hell is the most prevalent reality there is because most people, according to the Word of God, are going to wind up there. God commanded Ezekiel to <u>warn</u> the wicked of their way, yet we try to persuade them in a nicer approach so that we don't offend them.

God has said that it is by the fear of the Lord that men depart from evil, but many tell us that it is by the "love" of God because that is what they've been taught to believe. We are often led by what we want to hear and, as a result, by what we have figured out, not by the depth of the Spirit and the Word of God.

Our great revivals in the past have shown us that when people are shown the reality of Hell, then Holy Ghost conviction will bring them to the Cross in great numbers. Even today, when we see plays such as "Heaven's Gates and Hell's Flames," we see large numbers of people come to the altar to repent because the reality of an eternity in hell has gripped their souls. In too many cases, however, we return to our old, comfortable ways as soon as the presentation is over.

Don't we get it? Sure, it's an old-fashioned gospel, but since when has God changed His message? But this is a more modern age, isn't it, and our churches today have a very different approach, a different message, and, predictably, very different results.

If that is not so, where is the fruit, the reaping of lost souls? How many people got saved at your church last week? How about last month? I'm not talking about Christians coming down to the altar week after week for the same old things that they can never seem to get victory over.

And I'm not talking about you gaining church membership from the dead wood of some other dead church. I'm talking about lost souls coming under Holy Ghost conviction, coming to a place of repentance before God, and surrendering their hearts and souls to Him. That's the fruit that you're supposed to be bearing. Remember that the Lord cursed the fig tree for not having fruit on it, even though it was not in season. There were no excuses.

Fear: We see an emphasis in many of the churches today on a "Love" gospel. The fear of God is minimized and often villainized for scaring people.

The Word of God says that "perfect love casts out all fear," true, but the Lord was not contradicting himself here. The Fear of God is the foundation upon which everything else rests.

There is no love without the fear of God because love is the keeping of God's commandments (John 14:21, 1st John 5:3, 2nd John 1:6), which is impossible without the fear of the Lord. The Word of God says that men depart from evil by the fear of the Lord (Prov. 16:6).

Wisdom, the "principal thing," *is* the fear of the Lord (Job 28:28). It made Jesus of quick understanding (Isaiah 11:3) and will do the same for you.

<u>Satanic</u> fear is what is cast out when you have the holy boldness that only comes through the fear of God.

Lest we succumb to a sophisticated definition of the word fear, remember that Moses hid his face because he was afraid to even look at God. David, the "apple of God's eye," feared God so much that the flesh on his bones trembled (Ps. 119:20), as did Paul's (Phil. 2:12). The great prophets of God spoke of the fear of the Lord in terms of "dread" (Isaiah 8:13). This is not the "awesome respect" that we hear our ecclesiastical scholars and preachers speak of today.

If the fear of God is so important, according to the Scriptures, why is it not emphasized in our churches? Is it because it is not a comfortable message, and we would rather hear about "smooth" things (Isaiah 30:10)?

If we do not preach a strong Gospel, we will not have a strong congregation, and our parishioners will not have the strength to stand in the day of temptation that is coming to try the whole earth. Like it or not, the dark days of spiritual famine <u>are</u> coming, and we will need the strength that comes from a strong stand in the depth of the Spirit to make it through those times. That comes from a walk with God that is strengthened and driven by the Fear of God.

Don't be fooled by a popular "love" gospel. The Word says to "behold the goodness <u>and</u> the severity of the Lord." (Romans 11:22)

Souls of men: The great focus of our churches today is on ourselves. We are so enamored with our own spiritual needs that we have forgotten our first love. Altar calls for the lost have been replaced with calls for church members to get prayed over for everything from a sore foot to a new job. I see people coming up to the altar to get prayed over for the same troubles week after week, but are never able to get the victory, never able to overcome, never able to receive the strength to stand. All the while, souls are dropping off into an eternity of Hell with no hope of ever getting out, and no one is cut to the heart. We say we are, but talk is cheap.

Faith is action. I learned a long time ago that when you have problems, go take care of someone else's problems, and yours will dissipate like smoke. How many of us are storming the Throne of God for the lost? How many of us are taking the battle to the streets and witnessing our hearts out? Where are the old-fashioned warriors of old? The ultimate goal of Christianity is to win souls. When we lose sight of that, we lose our focus on God, and we lose our power in Him.

The prophet Amos cried out against the Church, "Woe to them that are at ease in Zion" (Amos 6:1) Who is Zion? Is that not the Church? And are we sitting at ease in our complacency toward winning the lost? As Amos accuses us later on in the same chapter, that we are not "grieved for the affliction of Joseph." In other words, we are not cut to the heart that souls are cascading into Hell. And as a result, we will be the first to go into captivity (Amos 6:7), because judgment will begin at the house of God.

Joel also points the finger at us when he says, *"Be ye ashamed, O ye husbandmen; howl, O ye vinedressers, for the wheat and for the barley; because the harvest of the field is perished.*" (Joel 1:11) The harvest of souls has been left to rot in the fields as millions drop off into an eternity of Hell ... and God blames us.

When a church is not focused on winning the lost, it has disregarded the one last request that Jesus gave us just before He left. His one last request had nothing to do with church activities or church growth, giving food to the poor, or developing ministries that only minister to the saved.

"Go," He said, "into all the world, and preach the gospel to every creature." (Mark 16:15). Go. Not sit. "How beautiful are the <u>feet</u> of them that preach the gospel of peace," not the <u>behinds</u> that sit in the pews.

Find these four things in a church, and you will find the presence of God. If they are missing, it will be hard to find that vibrancy that fuels the Holy Ghost fire you are looking for.

Sons of Sceva

> *Then certain of the vagabond Jews, exorcists, took upon them to call over them which had evil spirits the name of the Lord Jesus, saying, We adjure you by Jesus whom Paul preacheth. (Acts 19:13)*

It always sounds so easy. Just say the words, clap your hands twice, click your heels, and kazaam!

I am so tired of hearing that all we have to do is speak positive words, and it will bring life or blessings or healing or whatever we are trying so desperately to believe. But that isn't faith talking; that's presumption. Motivational speakers may sound inspiring and fill you with neat sayings that make you feel good, but that doesn't make them prophets of God. The power of positive thinking does not equate to the power of the Holy Spirit.

Those sons of Sceva in the above chapter of Acts saw all the miracles that Paul did and naturally figured that if they did the same things and said the same words that they would get the same results. Except they were missing the one thing that made all the difference – the power that only comes through a crucified walk before God in deep, broken subjection to the Spirit of God. Everyone wants to be a prophet, but no one wants to pay the price.

Instead, we grasp for shortcuts in our lives. We hypothesize. Just say the words, and it will come to pass. "This will be your year of blessings and prosperity ..." Oh, wait a minute. Didn't we hear that *last* year? And the year before?

Or how about this? "Call those things which be not as though they were ..." (Rom. 4:17). And so we run around speaking things into the air to make them happen. Look at that passage carefully. God never gave us the power of creation to speak words of power to make things happen. That's not faith; that is sorcery. You go to Hogsworth to learn that.

Faith has to be built (Jude 1:20); it is not wished into being. And there is a price for it, just as there is a price for everything in God. Anything other than that is just wishful thinking and will not produce lasting and full results. Every great man or woman of God had their 40 years in the backside of a desert before they were ever brought forth by God to exercise His power.

Ah, but that's not what we want to hear, is it? We want everything to be quick 'n' easy in our microwave society. Snap your fingers and be healed!

And the demon taunted back to the sons of Sceva, "Jesus I know, and Paul I know; but who are ye?"

He knew who Paul was. Paul was famous in hell! Why? Because Paul, unlike Sceva's lightweight sons, had paid the price in blood, tears, and prayer. He had stormed the gates of hell armed with a faith that had been built one block at a time, and he had declared victory in the blood of Jesus Christ over everything Satan had thrown at him. Oh yes, that demon knew who Paul was … and he feared.

But empty words of presumption based on a theological faith without any price, blood, or effort will not turn back the tides of darkness. Faith is built one precept at a time, and power in God is brought forth out of the crucified depths of prayer. There is a price for power in God, and it is not cheap, nor is it easy.

That is why we see so many false prophets running around the church today, like Pied Pipers declaring all the things that our itching ears want to hear (2 Timothy 4:3). Our church world has become little more than a revolving social circuit of entertaining speakers proclaiming great swelling words of encouragement to a church that, instead, is in desperate need of repentance. Instead of bringing us into the fear of the Lord, they are leading us in the power of positive thinking. In doing so, they are leading us away from the altar of repentance, which is the one place we need to be to see revival.

> *For the kingdom of God is not in word, but in power. (1 Corinthians 4:20*

What is the Fullness of Joy?

"Joy to the world, the Lord is come, Let earth receive her King"

Joy is one of those simple 3-letter words that you don't often take the time to think about, but when I did, I realized that I wasn't sure that I fully understood what the fullness of Joy really is. It isn't just happiness. Any circus clown can be happy. Joy goes deeper than a white painted face, a red bulb nose, and long floppy shoes. Joy is the music of the soul when it is rejoicing.

There are plenty of references to joy in the Bible. The shepherds had it on Christmas morning, as did the man who found a treasure in the field. The angels have it every time a sinner repents. In the presence of God, there is fullness of joy. And when you believe, there is joy unspeakable and full of glory.

Joy has a voice, but it is not confined to singing, laughter, or celebrations. It often comes forth out of sorrow. We can leap for joy when we are persecuted and then break forth in joy when we are delivered. A woman has sorrow at the time of her travail, but great joy when her child is born. The churches in Macedonia had joy during great trials of affliction, and Paul joyed and rejoiced over the prospect of being sacrificed for the church (Col. 1:24). Obviously, joy issues forth out of wells that are deeper than just surface happiness. There is pain associated with Joy.

Joy finds itself at the center of many of our endeavors. I believe that the dynamic between pain and joy is where passion is born. It is a fountain that brings a reason for why we do anything. If not for joy, why would we work, fight, strive, or push to accomplish our goals in life? It is the fuel that drives us. Joy is an essence of life that creates the same difference between life and living as there is between church and revival.

The thing that really gets me, however, is the idea that for the joy that was set before Him, our Savior gladly endured the cross so that we could be saved. That places joy in a much deeper dimension than some emotional feeling. What is this joy that slips past all attempts to describe it, that is not confined to human emotions, that pulls from the depths of pain and agony to give birth to a victory that transcends the limits of Eternity?

I can only come up with one answer. Joy is a gift that God has given us to fuel our passion to immerse ourselves in the Love of God.

As the hart panteth after the water brooks, so panteth my soul after thee, O God. (Psalms 42:1)

Daniel's Final Mission

Belshazzar the king made a great feast to a thousand of his lords, and drank wine before the thousand.

Belshazzar, whiles he tasted the wine, commanded to bring the golden and silver vessels which his father Nebuchadnezzar had taken out of the temple which was in Jerusalem; that the king, and his princes, his wives, and his concubines, might drink therein. (Daniel 5:1,2)

Sheer rebellion. We look back now and can clearly see Belshazzar's utter foolishness in defying God, but at the time, he was the guy in power, and he sure seemed to be bulletproof. After all, the mightiest army on Earth had just left and given up the siege around Babylon. Where were those rumors now that there would only be three generations to Nebuchadnezzar's reign in Babylon? Cyrus was gone. The great Babylon was impregnable! They were stronger than God!

And then came the writing on the wall ...

Daniel was an old man by now. Under Belshazzar's grandfather, Nebuchadnezzar, Daniel had been a man of great authority in charge of the affairs of state for this great empire. He was a man much sought after for his wisdom and his eerie ability to understand mysteries and dreams. He had a personal connection with God that even the king respected. But not Belshazzar.

Character and integrity are not always passed on to subsequent generations, and Nebuchadnezzar's grandson, although aware of his grandfather's humbling experience with God, refused to submit to God. He heard Daniel's warning from the Hebrew prophet Jeremiah that he would be the last of Nebuchadnezzar's line (Jer. 27:7), but he laughed at it. And now Cyrus, Babylon's greatest threat, had been defeated, and just to show his arrogance and defiance, Belshazzar would bring out the sacred vessels and have a drunken party for a thousand of his lords.

Daniel, who had been set out to pasture, was in his 70's or 80's by now. He knew the time was nigh for the fulfillment of the restoration of Jerusalem that would come after years of captivity. He had served well during those years, but how long it had been! But he would have one more mission for God, his greatest one. He knew the prophecy in Isaiah 44 and 45 very well. Whether he understood the details was not important. That which God had promised, He would bring to pass. And somehow this revelation had been handed to Daniel to be brought forth at the right time.

And now the queen was calling for him to come into the banquet room to tell the king what the writing on the wall meant.

God does not move according to our time schedule. I guess you already knew that. There is a three-part process that sometimes takes so long you wonder if it will truly ever come to pass. But God says that he that comes to God has to first believe that He is and that He is a rewarder of them that diligently seek Him (Hebrews 11:6). The prayer, the promise, and the fulfillment -- You pray until you get an answer, and then you wait for it to happen – and it always takes longer than you expected.

How long did Daniel wait? When was the prophecy first revealed to him? Did he know that he could not die until he met Cyrus? Did he stand inside the banquet room to point at the handwriting on the wall and then show this new king the ancient prophecy in the Holy Scriptures that had Cyrus' name clearly written along with a full description of exactly how he would conquer Babylon? Did Cyrus the new king turn slowly to look at that handwriting and feel a cold chill come across him that it was God, not Cyrus, that had conquered this city?

They say that God moves in mysterious ways. I suppose that's true. I, for one, have quit trying to figure out what He is doing. I often joke that I subscribe to the Alfred E. Newman philosophy from Mad Magazine, *"What, me worry?"* It's a whole lot simpler to just let God be God. He does a pretty good job of it when He is free to do things His way. Just let me get out of the way.

Sometimes, we put a time limit on God. We toss our prayers out there, click our heels three times, and expect to be back in Kansas. And when the answers to those prayers fail to materialize, is that a failure of God's timing or a failure of us to pray until we get a real answer? Do you pop out 60-second snapshot prayers and expect God to jump to your rescue, or do you contend before God, grab hold of the horns of the altar, and continue to cry out to God until you feel that anointing come down with that sweet knowledge that you know that you know that your prayer is answered? That kind of victory in prayer gives you a grip on an answer that is sure for Eternity. Without that, all you have is a case of wishful thinking ... and that is presumption, not faith.

Daniel was a man of prayer – three times a day – and yet he ruled the largest kingdom on Earth at that time. He made time to pray, and he sought the face of God until He answered him. That's why when Daniel prayed, God listened. If ever there was a man to choose for this incredibly important mission that would take 52 years to fulfill, it was Daniel. God chose wisely.

"But in the first year of Cyrus the king of Babylon the same king Cyrus made a decree to build this house of God." Ezra 5:13

Camper for Sale

Well, I was supposed to take the summer off, so I bought an old used travel trailer. The idea was that I would fix it up on the cheap and use it to have some fun this summer. I envisioned myself camping at the Brazos River or cruising around Colorado stopping to camp wherever I felt like it. I'd been waiting to be able to do something like that for a long time. I just needed money.

I had some silver saved from a previous deal to pay for the camper, but since the price of silver is so low, I decided to substitute the silver with the money I had stored away in the ministry account and pay it back later when the price of silver rose. Since I am a sole proprietor and not a corporation, legally, it didn't matter.

Sounded simple to me, but what a mistake that was!

Every time I turned around, there was another thing that needed to be fixed – reinforce the walls, replace the toilet, rebuild the wastewater plumbing, fix the lights, etc. Frustrating as it was, it was more like a hobby than a chore, but I had a nagging feeling that this whole thing was not being blessed. It was like I was struggling against the Lord to pursue what I wanted instead of what He wanted. I was still looking ahead to traveling across the countryside in my cute little trailer, but the price to do that kept going up.

Last weekend, however, was the last straw. We used the trailer to travel to a watermelon festival, only to come back to the RV park to find that the entire awning and some skylights had been destroyed by a sudden freak storm. That was it for me. It is now up for sale.

So, who were the invisible forces at work here? Which one was the devil, and which one was the Lord? I have always believed that when the devil is attacking, it may cost money, frustrate you, and drive you crazy, but you can always overcome it. When the Lord is working against you, however, you cannot. He always wins. But which one was working here?

I think it was both. I think, because of my slothfulness and slack principles, the Lord allowed the devil to have at me.

The Lord is mindful of diligence and attention to detail. I have noticed the same principle in wealthy people. Many of them seem to be diligent with small details, while many who are poor are not. That's a generalization, I realize, but I have found that to be mostly true. When I loosely considered swapping my silver for ministry cash, it seemed no big deal. I would swap it back later, and everything would be equal. But that is not how the Lord looked at it.

The Lord is a sharp Jewish businessman, and He is concerned with details. Small actions show our hearts. What we speak and do reflects our intentions and sets the course that we are about to travel. The Book of James says that if we can control the tongue, we can control the whole body. "How great a matter a little fire kindleth!" (James 3:5)

Spiritually speaking, we need to be concerned with the details of righteousness. Many people feel that because we are under grace, we don't have to worry about those little things, but I disagree. Those little things are what determine your destiny.

- "The little foxes, that spoil the vines" (Song of Songs, 2:15)
- "He that is faithful in that which is least is faithful also in much" (Luke 16:10)
- "The slothful man roasteth not that which he took in hunting: but the substance of a diligent man is precious." (Proverbs 12:27)

The Lord does pay attention to details, and He demands a holy people to do the same. It's not for His benefit, but for ours so that we can be blessed in Him and prosper for our obedience and attention to details of righteousness.

No, I'm not going to burn in hell for swapping money, but I sure learned a lesson. I was so focused on what I thought I wanted that He had to smack me upside the head for me to wake up. Thank God for the mercy of God.

Anyone interested in buying a camper? I have one for sale. Cheap.

"What, Me Worry?"

(Alfred E. Newman, Mad Magazine)

My mother hated *Mad Magazine*. She thought their hilarious spoofs would teach me to be irresponsible, unholy, and generally wayward. Alfred E. Newman, the flagship personality of the entire magazine was especially abhorrent to her. He would be the ruin of me if she allowed me to be exposed to his reprobate way of thinking.

So, I would stash my copies with my other contraband, like pocketknives and chewing gum. Poor Mom. She never suspected how corrupt I had become.

Years later, I have discovered that Alfred was not so far off the truth. His philosophy on life is echoed by the Apostle Paul, only in a much different context. Paul's repeated exhortation was to cast off your carnal worries and allow God to take control of your life.

> "Be careful for nothing..." (Philippians 4:6)
> "With food and raiment, therewith be content..."
> (1 Timothy 6:8)

"For I determined not to know anything among you, save Jesus Christ, and him crucified." (1 Corinthians 2:2)

Jesus echoed this same sentiment with, *"Fear not little flock, for it is your Father's good pleasure to give you the kingdom."*

So, what are we worried about?

I spoke to a wealthy young man last night about his concerns that his latest tithing was not bringing back the results he expected. Normally, he gives heavily, and there is an immediate response from the Lord in new deals and revenues, which he then, in turn, sows back into the ministries that he supports. This last time, however, he did not see the usual response from God, and he was getting worried about going broke. I might mention that he tithes over 50% of his income, and sometimes much higher.

I gave him my best impression of Alfred E. Newman. Don't worry about it because it really doesn't matter. If you're giving just to receuve, you're doing it for all the wrong reasons. If you're giving because you believe in this gospel, then it doesn't matter if you get anything back. If you want true prosperity, then you have to let go.

Prosperity is not measured in dollars and cents but in the lack of financial stress. Your ties with the things of this world have to be cut so that you, as Paul also put it, are crucified unto the world, and the world is crucified unto you. You no longer care. There is nothing in that world that you long for or lust for. The connection is severed, and your treasure is now in Heaven, not in this world.

It may be that the blessing you are not seeing is the stretching of your faith by allowing you to walk without the tangible crutch of money. Or food. Or home. Does it not say, "And having food and raiment let us be therewith content"? Food and clothing are the only things mentioned. And maybe God is doing that so your faith will grow as you learn to trust Him completely, enabling you to step up into a higher calling and a greater effectiveness than you have ever known ... and thereby greater blessings.

When we come to the realization that we are dead to this world and alive only in Christ, and when the world no longer has any pull on us because we are dead to it, we then enter into a crucified walk in God, broken to His will, and yielded to His purpose.

It is then that the cares of this life are sloughed off like a dead layer of skin, and we are truly free.

Cain and Abel

"And in process of time it came to pass, that Cain brought of the fruit of the ground an offering unto the LORD. And Abel, he also brought of the firstlings of his flock and of the fat thereof. And the LORD had respect unto Abel and to his offering..." Genesis 4:3,4

I used to think that the one big difference between Cain and Abel's offerings was the blood of the lamb – and that is still true – but there is another pointed difference that is brought out more in the original Hebrew than in the English, and that is the difference between the two men themselves.

Cain brought forth an offering which in itself was not intrinsically wrong; it was how he offered it. An offering, true, and a bit of a sacrifice, also true, but there was no great emotional cost, no great cutting to the depths of his soul. Those fruits that he offered could be regenerated, so the cost to Cain was minimal. Nice gesture, but just an offering. No big deal.

But Abel brought forth a firstling lamb. Not only would there be no regeneration from this lamb, but it was also a firstborn lamb, making it the first and strongest from that sheep and, therefore, the most valuable. He could have offered an older sheep that he had already gotten wool from or one that had already given birth to other sheep, but he purposely chose a lamb from which there was only cost, no profit. It was a total sacrifice. His heart cried out to offer a true sacrifice that would cut into his soul in order to reach out to God. His was the cost of blood. That was the real difference between Cain and Abel.

And so, we see that same difference in the natures of two kinds of Christianity today. One is content with church on Sunday and prayer meetings on Wednesday, while the other is broken at the altar of prayer, seeking the face of God for something more than just "church as usual." Don't get me wrong, church is good, but if that is all you want, then that is all you will get. A faith that has no cost in brokeness or tears is anemic and superficial at best and non-existent at worst.

Abel's faith went beyond the boundaries of duty and obligation to seek for an offering that had meaning, and so does the faith of those who strive to seek the face of God for more than the perpetuity of a church membership or the prolongation of a denominational order. They want God in person, the presence of His holiness in power, and His glory revealed in them. They want the real thing, and nothing else will do.

Like Cain, the church of complacency does not see herself the way that God sees her. She is the Church of Laodicea, content in the fullness of her sufficiency but blind to the realities of her spiritual bankruptcy and refuses to be ashamed. She sees her accomplishments as being substantial but is quick to accuse her brother Abel of his purity and zeal.

It is an established religion that always persecutes true Christianity. It has always been this way. It was the Pharisees and the Sanhedrin, not the Romans, who delivered Jesus to be crucified. It was the Roman Catholic Church, not the pagans, which slew millions of born-again Christians for their faith. The religious offspring of Cain has killed the prophets, burned Christians at the stake, imprisoned them, and tortured them all in the name of God. And they have done this, not to correct errant heresy, but to establish their own righteousness in a vain attempt to circumvent and escape repentance.

And so it is in these last days. We have great big churches filled with lights and music, celebration and praise. We praise our wonderful, loving pastors and the soft, unobtrusive welcoming we have for everyone. But there is no repentance, and, as Leonard Ravenhill once wrote, we have more of Hollywood than holiness.

I have been asked what kind of church I am looking for — one where God shows up at. Great music, emotional highs, charismatic oratory, fancy trappings, and smiling people do not constitute the presence of God. That's all nice, but it's all the result of human endeavors, not the result of the presence of the Holy Ghost.

Where are the souls getting saved? Where are the healing miracles? Where is the outpouring of the supernatural power of God? Where are the thundering messages of Holy Ghost conviction? Where can I find broken hearts of repentance in the presence of the absolute holiness of God? Where is the real thing?

When God is present, these things accompany Him. When these things are not present, neither is the Holy Spirit which brings them. But will the church of Cain acknowledge this? Have they ever?

God will give the churches a certain space of time to repent … and they will not repent. And then He will raise stones in their place. Revival is coming, but only to those who, like Abel, offer the firstling of the flock.

Gilbert Tennent
by David Smithers

"It is good for me that I have been afflicted; that I might learn thy statutes." (Psalm 119:71)

It was upon the bed of affliction that Gilbert Tennent was taught of God. In approximately 1728, this young, gifted Presbyterian minister became extremely ill. Uncertain if he would recover, he entered into a deep vision of eternity and a time of repentance. He writes, "I was then exceedingly grieved I had done so little for God . . . I, therefore, prayed to God that He would be pleased to give me one-half year more. I was determined to promote His kingdom with all my might and at all adventures."

Mr. Tennent's prayer was answered, and he was revived in both body and spirit. He labored as never before to "Sound the trumpet of God's judgment and alarm the secure by the terrors of the Lord." He was a man consumed with a vision of the holiness of God. As a result, he urgently warned the stubborn sinner and hypocrite of a final judgment and eternal hell. The anointed George Whitefield writes of him, "Hypocrites must soon be converted or enraged at his preaching. He is a son of thunder and does not regard the face of man. He is deeply sensible of the deadness and formality of the Christian church in these parts and has given noble testimonies against it." Gilbert Tennent preached as if "never sure to preach again and as a dying man to dying men." His preaching was far from typical of his day. A historian of the "Great Awakening" describes the average minister's methods, "The habit of the preachers was to address their people as though they were all pious and only needed instruction and confirmation. It was not a common thing to proclaim the terrors of a violated law and insist on the absolute necessity of regeneration."

Mr. Tennent himself describes this kind of popular preaching. "They often strengthened the hands of the wicked by promising them life. They comfort people before they convince them; sow before they plow: and are busy raising a fabric before they lay a foundation. These foolish builders strengthen men's carnal security by their soft, selfish, cowardly discourses. They have not the courage or honesty to thrust the nail of terror into the sleeping souls!" From 1736 through the 1740s, Gilbert Tennent's ministry was greatly blessed in promoting revival among the middle colonies in America. His ministry overlapped and supported the ministries of such godly men like Jonathan Edwards and George Whitefield. He carried with him the very seeds of revival, and when he preached, revival firefell. It must be remembered that the American church in the 18th century would probably have died of dry rot without the Spirit-filled ministry of Gilbert Tennent. During one of Boston's most severe winters, people waded through the snow night and day for the benefit of hearing the fiery Tennent preach. "You could criticize him, you could praise him, but you could not ignore him!" No one slumbered peacefully when he was around; not even the church. Gilbert Tennent was, in truth, the voice of one crying in the wilderness – REPENT!

He could boldly warn men of the wrath of God because he had boldly agonized and travailed for their souls, "Often his soul wept in secret for the pride and obstinacy of those who refused to be reclaimed." Throughout Tennent's ministry, he kept his zeal and love for Christ fervent through constant prayer. "He made prayer his chief and most delightful employment."

Proverbs 27:1 says, *"Boast not thyself of tomorrow; for thou knowest not what a day may bring forth.."* We have no promise of another day or even another hour, yet we too often live and breathe for the things of this world. What we desperately need is a revelation of eternity, of a real hell, and of a God who is to be loved and feared! If we truly had such a vision, we would not let one day go by without urgently warning the sinner and backslider. We would not let one hour go by without fervently praying for a true heaven-sent revival.

David Smithers

Where is the Wise?

> *Where is the wise? where is the scribe? where is the disputer of this world? hath not God made foolish the wisdom of this world? For after that in the wisdom of God the world by wisdom knew not God, it pleased God by the foolishness of preaching to save them that believe.*
>
> *For the Jews require a sign, and the Greeks seek after wisdom: But we preach Christ crucified, unto the Jews a stumblingblock, and unto the Greeks foolishness; But unto them which are called, both Jews and Greeks, Christ the power of God, and the wisdom of God. (1 Corinthians 1:20-24)*

Paul had a problem with these Greeks. They thought they were so smart that they were going to figure everything out. Everyone had their own ideas, but, like rambunctious little children on the playground, it only led to confusion and division. If the foundation for the Church of Jesus Christ was ever going to be established so that the light of this gospel could shine to the rest of the world, then this pride and arrogance would have to be purged. The problem was that everyone thought they were the ones who were right.

But it wasn't about who was right or wrong. It was about operating in a different dimension than the carnal world. It was about being in the Spirit and not being subject to the pride of carnal wisdom.

The world by wisdom, Paul cried to them, did not know God. So, God decided to use something that the world didn't know to save them. God decided to use preaching. The Jews could not receive that as being theologically correct, and the Greeks thought it was stupid. Instead of figuring out which religious rule it fit into, God threw away the rules. Instead of making analytical sense so that the Greeks could use their prestigious abilities of reason to figure it all out, God used the foolish, the weak, the base, and the despised to confound them. He used things that are not and things that do not hold substance in this world, that cannot be seen, felt, or handled to bring to nothing the things that our carnal minds can grasp. He used faith, which is the substance, not of the world but of invisible things, to save us.

For three chapters, Paul rips back the carnal covering of this world's reality to plead with the Corinthians to turn their thinking inside out. Instead of eating the fruit of the Tree of Knowledge that is desired to make one wise, he pleads with them to humble themselves and realize that God doesn't need their fleshly excellence. Instead, God uses a hidden wisdom that defies all reason, a wisdom that the natural man cannot understand, to bring about the great works of God.

How much like America they were! We are so theologically sophisticated that we have the arrogance to dismiss the Old Time Gospel as out-of-date and the hard message of hellfire and judgment as something wrong. This generation seems to think that they know better than those old-timers who carried the Cross through times of persecution, paid the price in deep prevailing prayer, and changed the fabric of our society. We are much more enlightened now, so much so that we have redefined the meaning of Grace and adjusted and smoothed out the sharpness of the cutting edge of the Word of God.

The rest of the world is viewed as dimmer lights to us. Europe is cold, Asia is, for the most part, unconverted, South America is Catholic, and Africa is primitive and poor. We still see ourselves as the same Light upon the Hill that the Puritans believed they were, and we are eager to usher the rest of the world into our new enlightened state. But are we?

I am reminded of King Ahaz's brand-new brass altar in 2nd Kings 16 that he copied from the king of Assyria. Oh, it was made with bright and shiny brass with a modern design and was much better than that old Brazen Altar of the Lord. So, he moved the Brazen Altar of the Lord over and put this shiny new brass altar in its place. It sure seemed like a good idea at the time to trade the old ways for the new ways, but new and modern is not always right and good. In a short while, that same king of Assyria overflowed the banks up to the neck of Jerusalem and almost destroyed Judah, just as Isaiah had prophesied (Isaiah 8:8). Was that not because of Ahaz's indiscretion? Is that not what we are doing when we choose a modern Gospel that is more to our liking than that hard message of righteousness and the fear of God?

I have one question for us – a litmus test, so to speak. If we are so good and the gospel that has evolved over the last 50 years with this modern generation is so much better, then, as Gideon once pointed out, where are all the miracles our fathers told us about?

Mark tells us that these signs will follow them that believe. (Mark 16:17-18). Then where are the signs? I'm not talking about weak-kneed excuses for the anemic show of faith. I am talking about the supernatural demonstration of the Spirit that Paul boasted of in 1 Cor. 2:4. Where are the healing lines where everyone gets healed? Where is the supernatural Presence of the Holy Spirit that fills the room like a cloud of righteousness, which makes the air shimmer from the glory of God and drives sinners to the altar in droves? Where are these signs that were once so abundant? We used to have them 50 years ago. Where are these supernatural signs today?

I see them in Africa. Yes, that same Africa that we patronize as if they were lesser lights and children in theological sophistication. And yet, God shows up in Holy Ghost power over there with miracles, healings, and revival. And we think we are somehow more enlightened than them?

Our grandfather's generation knew God in power and, like Paul, who gloried in the fact that he knew nothing except Christ Jesus and him crucified, they rested in their reliance on being led by the Spirit, not on their lexicons, outlined sermon notes, visual aids, smoke, and mirrors. No, they yielded in the pulpit and allowed the Spirit of God to preach the message. Something that we have lost the ability, courage, or faith to do anymore.

Only when we crucify our flesh, dispense with our carnal theological wisdom and our stubborn, rebellious ways, will we ever be able to humble ourselves and fully take on the mind of Christ. Only then will God allow us to enter into that place of true power in God.

And then, God will get all the glory, not us.

Thus saith the Lord, Stand ye in the ways, and see, and ask for the old paths, where is the good way, and walk therein, and ye shall find rest for your souls. But they said, We will not walk therein. (Jeremiah 6:16)

Drench the Sacrifice

And he put the wood in order, and cut the bullock in pieces, and laid him on the wood, and said, Fill four barrels with water, and pour it on the burnt sacrifice, and on the wood. (1Kings 18:33)

I spend a lot of time emphasizing the absolute need for reading the Word of God. There is no substitute for it. The Word of God gives us the power to be able to contend in prayer so we can reach the Throne of God; it gives us the strength to overcome sin and temptation, and it teaches us the wisdom, knowledge, or understanding to guide us in the path. But more than that, it feeds our souls and draws us close to God. There cannot be a revival without it.

Elijah called for four barrels of water to be poured on the sacrifice. Then he called for four barrels two more times. He poured it on the sacrifice until the water ran over into a ditch. The message to us is that we have to drench our sacrifice with the water of the Word of God before the fire of God will ever fall. There will be no revival without it. I have emphatically preached this message wherever I have gone, but yesterday, the Lord gave me the reason why revival is so dependent upon the Word.

If God were to send a revival to a people who were not immersed in God's Word, then they would not be able to nurture and raise the new souls that were coming in to get saved. How could they tell them what God expected of them if they hadn't read it in the Bible themselves? We spend so much time listening to others speak, we read all kinds of other books and watch videos, we spend so much time going to conferences, seminars, and meetings ... but we don't go to the Source and sit down to read the Word of God itself. Oh sure, we nibble at it, but do we devour the Word as if our lives depended on it? As a result, we have a majority of believers who are not empowered with the Word of God and, therefore, would not be able to sustain new souls that would come in if God sent them a true Holy Ghost revival. Those new souls would die — or worse, they would become just like us.

Satan knows this. He is intensely aware of how weak and susceptible to his influence a Christian is who does not have the depth and power that only comes from reading the Word of God. So, he works overtime to convince us that it is okay to listen to someone else, read someone else's book, or watch their video. "Moses, you go up the mountain and meet with God, and we will stay down here and buy your video for a Love offering of $19.95 when you come back down." Unfortunately, we end up worshipping golden calves instead.

In many of the places I go, there are few Bibles among the people. Even the pastors, especially out in the bush, are sometimes barely clinging to tattered Bibles held together with tape. How do you preach a strong message of revival and not provide them with the means to do it? What do we tell them? Be thou warmed and filled?

So, I buy hundreds of Bibles every year – as many as I can afford – and hand them out. It is never enough. Even when I filter out those who could buy a Bible but instead use their meager resources for other things like cell phones – necessary, yes, but not as necessary as the Word – there are still never enough Bibles to go around.

But their hunger is such that they snatch up whatever they can get from God. One church I went to had 45 members. Only the pastor had a Bible, and it was barely holding together. The way he would feed his flock was to pass the Bible around and let everyone read a portion and then pass it on to the next person to read. He did this, he said, so that everyone could "feel how good it is to read the Word of God."

Wow. Tell me that doesn't grab your heart.

Dear God, inspire us to rise to the challenge of Mordecai so that we do not hide behind the palace walls of wealth and prosperity but that we look over the palace walls to our brethren who are in such need and do what we can to sustain them. I am not talking about an entitlement program where you mindlessly send a check just to assuage your conscience, but a serious effort in prayer and support.

Here is the kicker. I believe that God's last great revival will begin in Africa. Oh, I know many of you think it will rise first in the USA, but America is nowhere near as desperately hungry for revival as Africa is. We are the Church of Laodicea — much too comfortable and unwilling to pay the intense price that is required for a real revival. Neither are we inclined to break to our knees in deep, brokenhearted repentance for the apostasy that is so rampant amongst us. According to that same passage, we do not even realize how far we have fallen. *"… and knowest not that thou art wretched, and miserable, and poor, and blind, and naked:"* (As far as we can see, we have a wonderful church. It's the <u>other</u> guy's church that needs to repent.)

If that is true – and I don't think there is any doubt about it – then what we do to support the church in Africa will ultimately reflect upon the church in America. And what we do <u>not</u> do will also reflect upon what mercy the Lord will or will not have upon us.

> *Whoso stoppeth his ears at the cry of the poor, he also shall cry himself, but shall not be heard. (Proverbs 21:13)*

Under a Bushel

I read this passage today as if it was the first time that I had seen it:

> *No man, when he hath lighted a candle, covereth it with a vessel, or putteth it under a bed; but setteth it on a candlestick, that they which enter in may see the light. (Luke 8:16)*

Obviously, this is talking about being a witness to the world. When you are saved, you receive the Light of the World, and you want to shine that Light in the darkness so that everyone can see the truth about salvation. You don't cover it up inside your vessel to hide it. Neither do you put it under your bed because you are too lazy to get up and shine the Light. You put it on a candlestick or lampstand so everyone can see.

But then He follows up with this next verse:

> *For nothing is secret, that shall not be made manifest; neither anything hid, that shall not be known and come abroad. (Luke 8:17)*

What is the connection here? Could it be that the Lord is warning us that when we refuse to obey

His commands to be a witness to the world, our sin will not be hidden? God sees and will make it manifest on the Day of Judgment.

And then He follows up with something very chilling:

Take heed therefore how ye hear: for whosoever hath, to him shall be given; and whosoever hath not, from him shall be taken even that which he seemeth to have. (Luke 8:18)

Just before Jesus left to ascend into the heavens, He had one last request. It wasn't to build ministries, hand out canned goods, be nice to everyone, or get wrapped up in a myriad of "church" things. It was simple: go win souls. Make disciples. Go into the entire world and preach the Gospel. All those other things may be good, but that's not what He told us to do. We seem to be doing everything else except what He asked us to do.

Could the Lord be warning us that those who faithfully follow His command to win souls will be given blessings, but those who do not will lose what they seem to have? What do they "seem" to have that they can so easily lose?

When we look at the parables of the Sheep and the Goats in Matthew 25, the Good Samaritan in Luke 10, the Church of Ephesus in Revelations 2, the

True Vine in John 15, and many other places, we see a severe warning that we will be judged, not according to our "church" works, but according to whether we had mercy on the lost or not. That was the only difference separating the sheep and the goats. It was the difference between the Good Samaritan and the priest and Levite. It was the one thing that kept your branch from drying up and being broken off to throw in the fire. Could it be that if we settle back and rest in our salvation like those who are at ease in Zion, thinking that we do not have to worry about facing a reckoning for our lack of mercy, the salvation that we "seem" to have is lukewarm and has no real substance to it?

I know everyone wants to think that everyone is going to Heaven, and that because we believe in Jesus and go to church that we will escape Hell. But read carefully, my friend. The warnings are all through the Bible … if you take time to see them.

> *If thou forbear to deliver them that are drawn unto death, and those that are ready to be slain; If thou sayest, Behold, we knew it not; doth not he that pondereth the heart consider it? and he that keepeth thy soul, doth not he know it? and shall not he render to every man according to his works? (Proverbs 24:11-12)*

But if the watchman see the sword come, and blow not the trumpet, and the people be not warned; if the sword come, and take any person from among them, he is taken away in his iniquity; but his blood will I require at the watchman's hand. (Ezekiel 33:6)

And he said, Unto you it is given to know the mysteries of the kingdom of God: but to others in parables; that seeing they might not see, and hearing they might not understand. (Luke 8:10)

By the Brook Cherith

We all cycle through the different contrasts of life – prosperity and poverty, laughter and tears, sickness and health. We're told that it is all designed to make us strong, stretch our character, and turn us into better people. That all sounds great if you plan on joining the U.S. Marines, but it is little comfort when you are dipping into the down part of that cycle. Even when you know how the drill works, it would be so much better if you got a word of encouragement from the Lord that you're okay, you're not being punished for something you did wrong, and you didn't zig when you were supposed to zag.

These past few months, I have felt like everything around me was shutting down. The finances were drying up, both personal and ministry. Opportunities to share the message God gave me were closed. I could not get any traction in the churches here in America. No one was interested beyond giving me their heartfelt "ataboy." I couldn't even give away the books that I had written. Plenty of people thought everything we put out in articles, newsletters, books, YouTube broadcasts, and

Facebook posts were great. They just weren't interested.

I needed an answer from God. I felt like I was sinking in quicksand.

So, He woke me up at 1:20 a.m. to go down and pray. Typical middle-of-the-night call to prayer. (It makes you wonder if He lives in an opposite time zone than ours. Or is it so that He can get our attention?) For the next 2 ½ hours, He unfolded His plan to me.

Elijah is the prophet that I most relate to. His message is the same as mine, and I see in his ministry a foreshadowing of the timeline for the last days. His ministry has six stages, and the Lord began to match them up with what was going on in my life.

Elijah began his mission by declaring the word of the Lord as a call to repentance. He appeared before both King Ahab and Queen Jezebel – the secular government and the established apostate church – and declared a spiritual famine for Israel. There would be neither dew nor rain until he said so. Beyond the physical drought, it was a spiritual drought, much like the famine declared by the prophet Amos in Amos 8:11. Against the backdrop of a lush countryside with plenty of rain and rivers flowing, Elijah's call for repentance fell on deaf ears.

I have had the same message – a call to the

church for broken-hearted repentance for being inwardly focused and full of "church" instead of going out to win the lost. The passages that point to severe judgment for not having mercy on the unsaved are numerous – so numerous that it takes me at least an hour to share them all with a congregation. But in America, I get the same response that Elijah got with Ahab. Even Jezebel, who hated the people of God, must have only been slightly bothered because although she had slaughtered the prophets, she only dismissed Elijah.

Who else are you going to preach to? Who will listen to you? Where are the real Christians who understand the spiritual devastation we are in? The answer comes back in hollow echoes – no one.

And so, it is off to the second stage: the Brook Cherith. No one to preach to, no one to warn, no direction to work toward, no vision to inspire and direct you. Did Elijah wonder what happened to him? He was part of a vibrant ministry, but now he has no idea what will happen next. The only ones he could ask these questions to were the ravens, who could only give an unintelligible squawk back to him.

The church didn't support him because the true church was missing. The carnal church that inhabited the land worshipped a different god. They thought Baal was the real god. After all, he gave them a much more modern and easier gospel than the old-fashioned Jehovah. This renegade Elijah and his strict, judgmental, fearful god had no place in their modern society.

It is noteworthy that it was ravens, not doves, that brought the bread and flesh to sustain Elijah. It was dark-feathered outsiders that kept Elijah alive, not the church. God provided a way that no one would have expected.

It struck me that the same thing happens to those who deliver the same message. They deliver warnings about the drought to the Court and have been dismissed. They have found no traction in America for this message, yet it is the same message that Elijah and John the Baptist brought. It is too hard, too strict, too judgmental. The strange thing is that while many pastors and evangelicals acknowledge that the message is true and have seen the incredible results in other places where this message has been preached, no one wants these Elijah-type preachers to rock the boat in their church here in America.

So, we are off to the Brook Cherith, where we are sustained by some brothers who are outside the traditional church.

The Lord showed me that this is what Elijah

had experienced at the Brook Cherith. While everything seems to be shutting down, it's not that the ministry has failed; it's that the brook is drying up, and we are about to enter the 3 ½ year period of the end times.

We're fed with enough to keep us going, but the intensity of ministry is over for right now. The Lord spoke to me in 1993 concerning what was coming. He said, "There yet remaineth an appointed time." That time appointed is found in Daniel chapter 11. It is still yet to come, but for now, I am watching the brook slowly trickle down to nothing.

It is time to move into the next phase - Zarephath.

Elijah is sent outside Israel, into the Gentile world of Sidon. This is not the church. This is completely outside the church. He will spend 3 ½ years with the widow of Zarephath with a little bit of meal (the Word of God) and a little bit of oil (the Anointing). This is a picture of the suppressed church during the 3 ½ years of the end time. Nothing is heard from Elijah. As a matter of fact, he cannot be found. Ahab is on a rampage looking for him, but the Lord has hidden him.

"Come, my people, enter thou into thy chambers, and shut thy doors about thee: hide thyself as it

were for a little moment, until the indignation be overpast." (Isaiah 26:20)

The modern church has rejected the holiness and righteousness of the Word of the Lord in favor of the enticements of Baal. She is becoming invisible to the Lord because she looks just like the world. Her garments are dripping with pearls and jewels, and her dress and mannerisms are like the wealth of this world. She looks like the world, sounds like the world, and even smells like the world. She is wooed by a lover who is not her husband, and she is becoming more and more infatuated with him. Jesus is losing His Bride, and oh, how His heart must be broken!

"Love not the world, neither the things that are in the world. If any man love the world, the love of the Father is not in him." (1st John 2:15)

We are in a spiritual famine, but she does not see it. The Church thinks she is doing great and will become the Church Triumphant. She is waiting for God to drop this great revival on her as she rises victorious over the darkness of this world. But the truth is that she has been blinded and is no longer able to recognize how far she has fallen.

(Because thou sayest, I am rich, and increased with goods, and have need of nothing; and

knowest not that thou art wretched, and miserable, and poor, and blind, and naked: (Rev. 3:17)

The Lord once spoke to me about the Church, *"I will give the churches a certain space of time to repent … and they will not repent. And then I will raise up stones in their place."* That is a direct quote, word for word. Those "stones" can be found in Joel chapter 2.

The fourth phase is the judgment on the Church on top of Mt. Carmel. Elijah calls down fire on the sacrifice and slaughters the priests of Baal at the Brook Kishon. It is not Ahab that is judged. It is the Church – the religious priests of the commonly accepted religion of the society. I don't know what form the judgment upon us will take, but I am assured that it will affect our entire society and will be worse than the disaster of 9/11. It will pull the carpet out from under the feet of the church to bring her to repentance. The prosperity that has wooed her away from her Bridegroom will be destroyed by fire. Revival cannot come unless there is a broken repentance that drives us to our knees, and it will take a severe judgment to break us to that point.

And then, there is a sound of an abundance of rain, the sound of a coming revival, the greatest revival of all time.

"Be glad then, ye children of Zion, and rejoice in the LORD your God: for he hath given you the <u>former rain</u> moderately, and he will cause to come down for you the rain, <u>the former rain, and the latter rain</u> in the first month." Joel 2:23

If the former rain was Pentecost, then a Second Day of Pentecost is coming that will be far greater than the first. The rain that comes drenches everything. This will be the greatest revival of all time.

Revival always comes after judgment and subsequent repentance. Without repentance, nothing will change. The whole purpose of judgment is to turn us back to God.

Revival is then followed by the persecution. After the rain, Jezebel, the Whore Church, rose up against Elijah to kill him. Jezebel was afraid of Elijah because she knew he had the power to destroy her. Instead of attacking him immediately, she gave him 24 hours to get out of town.

God then brings Elijah to Mt. Horeb to meet with Him.

"And he said, I have been very jealous for the LORD God of hosts: for the children of Israel have forsaken thy covenant, thrown down thine altars, and slain thy prophets with the sword; and I, even

I only, am left; and they seek my life, to take it away." 1ˢᵗ Kings 19:10

Forsaken thy covenant – the Church no longer adheres to righteousness and holiness in the fear of the Lord.

Thrown down thine altars – the Church is no longer what it once was. The altars that were once a place of repentance, tears, and brokenness have become a place for "pity lines" to pray for the things you didn't overcome last week and wishing wells where all you have to do is come down to the altar, and you will magically receive your gift.

Slain thy prophets – the prophets of God are no longer welcome. They have been replaced with modern prophets whose message is about love, blessings, and prosperity. Their messages are never about repentance. Their purpose is to keep the people of God away from the altar of repentance because Satan knows that without repentance, there can be no revival. So, they tell the people what they want to hear to make them feel good about themselves.

"For the time will come when they will not endure sound doctrine; but after their own lusts shall they heap to themselves teachers, having itching ears;" 2ⁿᵈ Timothy 4:3

And they no longer have to worry about being accurate in their prophesyings because they can *"prophesy according to the proportion of faith"* (Romans 12:6). How convenient. That frees them to prophesy whatever wispy thought enters their mind.

"I have heard what the prophets said, that prophesy lies in my name, saying, I have dreamed, I have dreamed." Jeremiah 23:25

<u>And I, even I only, am left</u> – That's what it feels like sometimes. Nobody understands you. You are on a solitary walk, and you do not fit in anywhere. You're not supposed to. You don't fit in the churches. Neither are they packing the stadiums to listen to the message that the Lord has given you. And yet, you know it is the Word of the Lord to this generation.

"Therefore, thou shalt speak all these words unto them; but they will not hearken to thee: thou shalt also call unto them; but they will not answer thee." Jeremiah 7:27
"And he said, Verily I say unto you, No prophet is accepted in his own country." Luke 4:24

The answer from God cannot be heard in the wind, the fire, or the earthquake. That's what most of us expect, but God bypasses the noise and celebration to speak clearly, quietly, and deeply to our hearts. Elijah recognizes that still, small voice. It is a voice that is as powerful as any shouting, but it is still, without the acoustic vibrations of sound.

This time, the response will be different. Just as the spirit of Elijah was upon John the Baptist, so will it also be on Joel's Army (Joel 2:1-11). It is the voice crying in the wilderness to prepare the way of the Lord and make straight in the desert a highway for our God. (Isaiah 40:3).

About the Author

Dalen Garris has been in ministry since 1970 during the Jesus Movement in California. In 1997, he began a radio broadcast that ultimately spread to dozens of countries, from Israel and Saudi Arabia to Africa and the Philippines. His program, *Fire in the Hole*, was selected for broadcast across North America on the Sky Angel network as the Voice of Jerusalem.

A newspaper column followed, for which he has written over 700 articles, which have been published in local newspapers and Christian magazines in several countries. He has also written over a dozen books and several booklets.

Since 2004, he has been lighting the fires of revival in churches spread across sub-Saharan Africa. During the course of 17 years, he has preached in over 1,000 churches and has seen hundreds of them set on fire and explode with growth, and hundreds of new ones planted across Africa. Hundreds of people have been supernaturally healed during the healing lines that so often sprang up during these revival meetings, and tens of thousands have been saved. And the fires are still burning.

Because of his work across Africa, Dalen Garris was awarded an honorary Doctorate in 2017 by the Northwestern Christian University of Florida. He was also awarded the Brevet de Merite from the Vision Barza Grands Lacs coalition of churches.

Dr. Garris currently lives with his wife, Cindy, in Waxahachie and is still heavily involved with churches across Africa. His pressing hope is in seeing this powerful move of God in Africa ignite us here in America. He believes that this upcoming generation will be the Gideon Generation that will usher in this last, great revival that he has preached about for so many years.

If you would like Dr. Garris to speak at your church or organization, please contact us for times and schedules. We do not charge, nor will we ever charge, to preach the Gospel anywhere in the world.

Books by Dalen Garris:

Available at: www.Revivalfre.org/books

Four Steps to Revival
Do You Have Eternal Security?
Standing in the Gap – True vs. False Prophets
Two Covenants – Torah-based Faith vs. Grace
The Hub – 12 Secrets to Answered Prayer
Fire in the Hole

Revival Campaigns

The Kenya Diaries
A Trumpet in Nigeria
A Scent of Rain
Into the Heart of Darkness
Fire and Rain
Revival Campaigns in Africa – 2019
The Battle for Nigeria
A Light in the Bush
A Match in Dry Grass
Planting a Seed in Liberia
A Whisper in the Wind
Talking With the Women, by Cindy
Tanzania, A Rumbling Under the Mountain

A Voice in the Wilderness series:
vol. 1, The Journey Begins
vol. 2, the Early Years
vol. 3, Prophet Rising
vol. 4, Revival in the Wings
vol. 5, Sound of an Abundance of Rain
vol. 6, Watchman, What of the Night?
vol. 7, Mud and Heroes
vol. 8, Ashes in the Morning
vol. 9, Shaking the Olive Tree
vol. 10, Winds of Change
vol. 11, A Final Call
vol. 12, Superficial Shells

Booklets
*Available at: **www.Revivalfire.org/booklets/***
A Volcano in Cape Verde
Nigeria, 2012
Calvinism Critique

RevivalFire Ministries

PO Box 822, Waxahachie, TX 75168

dale@revivalfire.org

www.Revivalfire.org

www.ingramcontent.com/pod-product-compliance
Lightning Source LLC
Chambersburg PA
CBHW070448050426
42451CB00015B/3389